CATHOLICISM TO ENJOY
RATHER THAN ENDURE

CATHOLICISM TO ENJOY RATHER THAN ENDURE

LIFTING THE BURDEN OF CLERICALISM

Kevin Clarke

Copyright © 2023 Kevin Clarke

The moral right of the author has been asserted.

Apart from any fair dealing for the purposes of research or private study, or criticism or review, as permitted under the Copyright, Designs and Patents Act 1988, this publication may only be reproduced, stored or transmitted, in any form or by any means, with the prior permission in writing of the publishers, or in the case of reprographic reproduction in accordance with the terms of licences issued by the Copyright Licensing Agency. Enquiries concerning reproduction outside those terms should be sent to the publishers.

Troubador Publishing Ltd
Unit E2 Airfield Business Park,
Harrison Road, Market Harborough,
Leicestershire LE16 7UL
Tel: 0116 279 2299
Email: books@troubador.co.uk
Web: www.troubador.co.uk/matador

ISBN 978 1 80514 004 7

British Library Cataloguing in Publication Data.
A catalogue record for this book is available from the British Library.

Typeset in 12pt Garamond by Troubador Publishing Ltd, Leicester, UK

Matador is an imprint of Troubador Publishing Ltd

*For my family, past and present, and especially
Sophie Rose (tickly toes and tickly nose) –
ever young at 3 years, 8 months, and 26 days.*

CONTENTS

Introduction	ix

Part One: Councils of the Church — 1
1. Councils of the Early Church — 6
2. Councils of the Middle Ages — 17
3. Councils Following the Reformation — 34
   The Council of Trent — 34
   The First Vatican Council — 40
   The Second Vatican Council — 49

Part Two: What To Believe? — 91
4. God and Creation — 99
5. The Incarnation of Jesus — 121
6. Sin — 143
7. The Catholic Church — 160
   The Nature of the Church — 162
   Ministry in the Church — 168

	Authority in the Church	185
	The Papacy	203
	The Sensus Fidei	217
8.	The Mass	224
	In Conclusion	260
	Closure	274
	Bibliography	277

INTRODUCTION

I was baptised a Catholic as an infant and this continues to be a title to which I subscribe. However, I find myself increasingly at variance with the mindset of many of those in a position of authority and with their view of what constitutes the Church.

This seems to be thought of principally in its institutional aspect. An organisation that has its own set of rules, regulations and practices, and which is administered by bishops and run on a day-to-day basis by priests as the sole authorised instrument for dispensing the merits of Jesus Christ. An organisation that draws a clear line of distinction between those who are ordained and those who are not, with the former assuming responsibility for all aspects of Church life, and claiming the right to do so by virtue of Divine Authority.

Missing from this description is any mention of what being a follower of Jesus means in human terms.

A sense of being part of, and of belonging within, a diverse group of people in which the risen Jesus has encountered each individual in his or her own particular fashion and continues to draw us together to form a living community of faith, hope and charity.

And yet this was how the Church was described by over two thousand bishops from around the world who attended the Second Vatican Council ('Vatican II'). This was a Council that was specifically convened by Pope (now 'Saint') John XXIII in order to examine the nature and purpose of the Church and our effectiveness in responding to the signs and the needs of our own times.

The Council took place in St Peter's Basilica in Rome and ran from 1962 to 1965. The bishops recorded a near unanimous vote of approval on a wide range of ecclesial issues and their findings are contained in sixteen formally approved Council Documents. These have been described as an attempt to bring past traditions into the present and to provide a renewal for our time of all that is Catholic.

So what has been the outcome of Vatican II so far? The event itself attracted considerable media attention at the time but in my experience we received a limited amount of detail on the actual content of the discussions, and I would describe the official feedback ever since as 'purposely selective'. As a result, Vatican II has become little more than a distant memory for the vast majority of people who were alive in the 1960s and

Introduction

I suspect that later generations of Catholics may not even be aware that such an event ever took place.

For my part, it was not until the mid-1990s and a random decision to enrol on a theology course[1] that I became more aware of the extent and significance of what had been discussed and agreed. My only explanation for this is that despite the apparent show of support by the bishops during the Council, there are elements within our pastoral leadership whose continuing preference is to return to the way in which things were said and done previously, on grounds that they consider this to be unquestionably correct, and they are prepared to use their power and influence in the Church to stifle further discussions by appealing to notions of loyalty.

The focus of the opposition to Vatican II is the claim that a number of its findings represent a break in continuity with the past and therefore with essential elements of Catholic teachings. It is a break that is cited as the reason for most of the Church's present difficulties such as the continuing fall in Mass attendance, a shortage of vocations to the priesthood and religious life, and what is considered to be a growing indifference among the laity to a number of previously recognised and accepted teachings and practices.

The alternative view is that the findings of the

---

[1] 'Contemporary Theology in the Catholic Tradition' at Heythrop College, University of London.

Council can be traced back to the Church's earliest roots and therefore serve to endorse a need for change in order to modify or eliminate some of the more recent and debatable accretions to earlier traditions. The reason for the Church's present difficulties in this case is suggested as being because of the slowness or the unwillingness of our pastoral leadership to implement the Council's recommendations.

The result today is a Church that is not entirely at ease with itself. A perceived ambivalence within the hierarchy has created a void that is being publicly exploited by differing factions within the Church in order to promote their own particular view of what should and should not constitute ecclesial orthodoxy. We might perhaps be likened to the Gospel account of the kingdom that is divided against itself (see Mk 3:24) – and with potentially the same end result!

In my view, this is a situation that needs to be resolved as a matter of urgency. The findings of a General Church Council cannot simply be overlooked or treated as optional extras but need to be recognised as an essential part of the promise we were given by Jesus that we would always be guided by his Spirit. To deliberately ignore this guidance seems to me to represent an act of betrayal by those who presently aspire to a position of pastoral leadership as well as a betrayal of the trust that is attached to their office.

This is an accusation that does not come easily to

someone from a generation that was brought up to believe our pastoral leadership and everything we were taught by them pertaining to 'Holy Mother Church' was precisely as Jesus always intended it to be. I believe the time has come for those in a position of authority to realise that what so many people have ceased to have faith in is not God, but rather the human organisation that claims with divine authority to instruct us how to reach God.

They need to acknowledge also that a ruling 'clerical caste' can no longer presume to operate entirely in accordance with its own agenda and expect to remain unaccountable for its actions. Our present system of Church Governance reflects a cultural legacy, not a theological necessity. It is foreign to the *New Testament*, and serves to mask what should be the inner unity and single purpose of the whole of the people of God.[2]

My reason for writing this book is twofold. First, to commemorate the sixtieth anniversary of the start of the Second Vatican Council by providing a brief summary of the contribution that Church Councils have made over the centuries in the development of Christian Doctrine and the way in which we presently operate as the Church. I regard this as a subject that deserves to be better appreciated within the Church at

---

2   Michael Richards, *A People of Priests: The Ministry of the Catholic Church* (Darton, Longman & Todd, 1995), p61.

large and with particular reference to the most recent insights from Vatican II.

Secondly, I wish to highlight a number of Church teachings and practices that give me cause for concern because of the way in which they continue to be presented by our pastoral leadership. I regard this as one of the principal reasons to explain the current levels of defection from within the Church and our negative rating in society in general.

My aim is not to challenge traditional Catholic beliefs but rather the way in which these appear to have become distorted over time in their retelling and which can often seem to comprise little more than a litany of 'dos' and 'don'ts'. Moreover, conflicts that arise in the process of faith's self-understanding are not usually between a straight affirmation or a straight denial, but about meaning, about making sense of what it is that we profess to believe – about interpretation.[3]

The Second Vatican Council was convened to examine issues of this nature and, under the guidance of the Spirit, it identified a clear set of guidelines for us to follow. This was an exercise that was intended to involve the whole of the faithful, with each of us being called upon to play our part in the building of the Church with the benefit of the charisms we received at baptism.

---

3   Gabriel Daly, 'Faith and Theology' in *The Tablet*, April 1981, p446.

Sixty years on, the vast majority of us are still waiting for the opportunity to exercise our vocation as 'The People of God'.

PART ONE

COUNCILS OF THE CHURCH

The Church came into being when Jesus invited twelve of his closest disciples to become a visible means for his message to continue to be presented to as wide an audience as possible. It was an invitation that came with the promise that their efforts and the efforts of all future followers would be guided and supported by his Spirit.

The 'Twelve' were successful in overseeing the formation of local groups of believers, who would come together on a regular basis to reflect on the Scriptures and to 'break bread' in the manner Jesus had indicated. These individual communities maintained a close contact with one another in order to discuss matters of shared belief and to resolve issues of common interest or concern, and this eventually developed into a regular pattern of group meetings that became known as 'councils' or 'synods'.

One of the earliest examples of a Church Council is the *New Testament* account of a meeting of the Apostles in Jerusalem to determine which Jewish customs and practices (in particular, the Mosaic stipulation for male circumcision) should a non-Jew be required to accept in order to become a Christian? This was a question that St Paul and St Barnabas had encountered on their teaching travels and which had also become an issue of concern for some of the recent Jewish converts in Jerusalem. The summary verdict eventually pronounced by St Peter was that the message of Jesus had been addressed to everyone, not simply Jews, and therefore no undue added requirements or restrictions should be imposed on those wishing to become fellow believers (see Acts 15:2–35).

The words 'council' and 'synod' are derived from the Greek meaning: a coming together; an assembly; a meeting for a purpose that could be legislative or administrative, but with the intention of reaching a decision. In due course, a distinction began to emerge between meetings called to examine matters that were judged to be of importance to all groups of Christians and others where the topics were considered to be of a more local or temporary nature.

The former became known as 'Ecumenical Councils', taken from the Greek word '*oikonomia*' meaning 'the whole of the inhabited world' and signifying a meeting to which bishops representing the entire network of 'local Churches' would be invited to attend in order to reach decisions and issue authoritative guidelines for all Christians to follow. While the above-mentioned Council of Jerusalem can be seen to meet this criteria, it has never been officially referred to as ecumenical, which is a title that was not formally allocated until several centuries later.

COUNCILS OF THE EARLY CHURCH

The Council of Nicaea (AD 325)

The first formally designated Ecumenical Council took place in Nicaea, which is within the modern Turkish city of İznik and was convened (and paid for!) by Emperor Constantine. Its purpose was to resolve a dispute regarding the nature of the relationship between God and Jesus, which, for some time, had been a widely debated and divisive topic among Christians and had even led to outbreaks of violence between opposing exponents and their supporters.

At the centre of the controversy was an Egyptian priest named Arius, who held that because God was unique and transcendent, God's essence could not be shared by another or transferred to another as this could imply a division in God. Arius contended that Jesus was begotten of God in time, not from all eternity, and so as part of creation he was inferior to God but still greater than other human beings. He also argued that God could not take on a human form because this is composed of matter and is therefore a product that emanates from the realm of the profane.

To explain this latter assertion, there was a school of thought at the time known as 'Gnosticism' (from the Greek word for 'knowledge'), which adopted a dualistic method of interpreting reality by dividing human experience into a good and real realm of spirit, and a bad and illusory realm of matter. It held that these two realms came from different sources that were always at enmity with one another. It was also an elitist philosophy, which proposed that those with 'spiritual knowledge' (i.e. the Gnostics) would ultimately be saved by escaping from the body and material constraints, some others might be helped to achieve a similar release, but for the majority of humanity there was no possible hope of salvation.

To refute the claim by Arius of a diminished notion of Jesus's divinity as the Son of God, the Council of Nicaea asserted that Jesus was of one substance or being with God the Father, not simply of a similar substance and not created at a particular point in time, but eternally begotten of the Father. This upheld the divinity of Jesus and the absolute unity between the Father and Jesus as the means whereby the eternal God had personally entered into the historical condition of humanity in the person of Jesus of Nazareth.

The pivotal word used in this description was *homousios* in its Greek form, or *consubstantialis* as its Latin equivalent, meaning 'of the same being'. However, this choice of word did not receive the unanimous support of the bishops as it was not a biblical term and was therefore judged by some to be inappropriate. Also, the word itself was considered to be capable of different interpretations and might be taken to imply that both Father and Son were the same person but operating in different guises at different times.

The Arian debate continued well after the close of the Council but in upholding the full divinity of Jesus and the mystery of God's incarnation, Nicaea can be said to have been significant for two reasons. First, as Jesus was understood as a divine personage, there could be no doubting that his life, death and resurrection achieved its intended purpose; and second, if God was willing to assume a truly human nature and a physical form in the person of Jesus of Nazareth, this firmly ruled out the Gnostic proposition that all matter must be intrinsically flawed (but keep the notion of 'Gnosticism' in mind for future reference!).

As a point of note, the eventual decision reached by the Council Fathers at Nicaea was very much influenced by the strength of the lobbying from the laity who had remained closely involved with the discussions and eventual decision-making.

The Council of Constantinople (AD 381)

The bishops at this Council reconfirmed the one in being of the Father and the Son that had been agreed at Nicaea and then proceeded to expand on this definition by emphasising a 'Trinitarian framework' to incorporate the Holy Spirit. The finally agreed text was:

'We believe in one God, the Father all-powerful, maker of heaven and earth and of all things both seen and unseen.

And in one Lord Jesus Christ, the only begotten Son of God, begotten from the Father before all the ages, light from light, true God from true God, begotten not made, consubstantial with the Father through whom all things came to be;

for us humans and for our salvation he came down from the heavens and became incarnate from the Holy Spirit and the virgin Mary, became human and was crucified on our behalf under Pontius Pilate;

he suffered and was buried and rose up on the third day in accordance with the scriptures; he is coming again with glory to judge the living and the dead; his kingdom will have no end.

And in the Spirit, the holy, the lordly and life-giving one, proceeding forth from the Father, co-worshipped and co-glorified with the Father and Son, the one who spoke through the prophets;

in one, holy, catholic and apostolic church. We confess one baptism for the forgiving of sins. We look forward to a resurrection of the dead and life in the age to come. Amen.'[4]

It is immediately evident that this statement from Constantinople closely corresponds with the *Credo* we recite at Mass each Sunday. A result that the theologian and historian, Norman Tanner, has described as, '…a remarkable tribute to these early Councils'. And, as two additional points of note, this original prayer is seen to begin with 'We believe' rather than our now customary 'I believe' and whilst we generally refer to our Sunday faith recital as the Nicene Creed, it should more accurately be called the 'Nicene-Constantinopolitan Creed'.

The Council of Ephesus (AD 431)

The essential purpose of this Council was to refute the proposition that there were two separate persons in Jesus – one divine and the other human. This was a view that had arisen as a result of the refusal by the then Bishop of Constantinople (Nestorius) to describe Mary as 'Mother of God' (*Theotokos* or God-bearer). His claim was that she had only given birth to a man (*Christotokos*) in whom God dwelt.

---

[4] Referred to by Norman Tanner, *The Councils of the Church: A Short History* (Crossroad Publishing, 2001), p24.

The Council affirmed the single and complete unity of Jesus by recognising Mary's title as *Theotokos*, but the bishops reached a deadlock in seeking to find an appropriate formula by which to define this. The Council itself ended in disarray, but a suitable formula of union was later agreed that confirmed Jesus was 'one person with two natures of which one was divine and one was human'.

The Council of Chalcedon (AD 451)

As at Nicaea a century before, the eventual outcome of Ephesus did not totally eliminate ongoing disputes or prevent new propositions being introduced. One such new formulation was that Jesus began with two natures but retained only one of these after his incarnation – a proposition known as 'Monophysitism' (derived from the Greek: *mono* = one; *physis* = nature).

The Council rejected this assertion by confirming that there were two distinct natures united in the person of the 'God-man' Jesus. It then became the task, once again, for the bishops to formulate the manner in which the divine and the human natures were combined, drawing together the teachings from the previous Councils that Jesus is truly God and truly man, begotten from the Father in his divinity and from Mary as regards his humanity.

To assist the process of discernment, Pope Leo I ('the Great') dispatched two legates to attend the

Council and to deliver his considered judgement on the subject. As a result of this intervention, the formal definition that emerged from Chalcedon was that Jesus had two natures which:

> '...undergo no confusion, no change, no division, no separation: at no point was the difference between natures taken away by the union but rather the property of both natures is preserved and comes together into a single person and a single subsistent being; he is not parted or divided into two persons but is the one true and the same only begotten Son, God, Word, Lord Jesus Christ, just as the prophets taught from the beginning about him and as the Lord Jesus Christ himself instructed us, and as the creed of the Fathers handed it down to us.'[5]

In this somewhat wordy formulation, the Council of Chalcedon defined what is known as the 'Hypostatic Union' (from the Greek word *hypostasis* meaning 'individual' or 'person'), namely the union of the two distinct natures of God and man in the person of Jesus, who is at the same time 'true God and true man'. One wonders how many Catholics today have ever heard of this expression, and appreciate the way in which it supports many of the titles we are inclined

---

5   Ibid, p28.

to attribute to Jesus without giving them any serious thought.

It is sometimes suggested that the wording of the definition at Chalcedon was a compromise that reflected the least level of disagreement among the bishops rather than representing a definitive consensus, thereby leaving it to future generations to interpret what was intended. Also, the contribution by Pope Leo towards the final outcome is often promoted as being an indication of the primacy in theological matters, which was already being attributed to the Bishop of Rome, as the recognised successor in title to St Peter.

The Second Council of Constantinople (AD 553)

The Council was called by Emperor Justinian (527–565) to reaffirm the findings of the previous Council by once again refuting the claim that Jesus only had a single nature. This was considered necessary as the earlier claims of *monophysitism* continued to persist within some of the Christian communities in the Eastern part of the Roman Empire. Justinian's aim was to attempt to reconcile the Monophysites with the Chalcedonians.

The Third Council of Constantinople (AD 680–81)

An outgrowth of the earlier refuted claim of *monophysitism* was '*monothelitism*', which is derived from yet another Greek word, this time referring to a person's 'will'. The claim on this occasion was that even if Jesus had two natures, he only had one will, and this was indistinguishable from the will of God. This, too, was refuted by the bishops who pronounced that Jesus had both a divine will and a human will.

This seems an appropriate point at which to remind ourselves that what we now understand about Jesus was not simply 'known' in the Church from the outset. Under the guidance of the Holy Spirit, it took these six Ecumenical Councils and considerable prayer and debate to achieve our present understanding and resultant beliefs.

The Second Council of Nicaea (AD 787)

This Council was called to settle the so-called 'iconoclast controversy'. This was a long-standing dispute within the Church concerning the use of religious images (icons). Should they be considered idolatrous, could they be misleading or could they be inspirational?

The three hundred bishops who attended this Second Council in Nicaea agreed to legitimise the cult of icons, specifying that adoration was due to God alone but that icons of Jesus, Mary, angels and saints could nevertheless be venerated.

The Fourth Council of Constantinople (AD 869–70)

The Council was called to resolve a dispute between Pope Nicholas I (858–867) and Emperor Michael III, who had forced the incumbent patriarch of Constantinople (Ignatius) to resign and replaced him with his own choice (Photius). Pope Nicholas was opposed to this substitution and formally excommunicated Photius. He dispatched three papal legates to preside over a council in order to secure an agreement for the reinstatement of Ignatius – a task that was swiftly accomplished.

This would be the final Ecumenical Council of the early Church. All of the Councils up to this point had been held in locations in the Eastern (Greek) part of the Roman Empire and were attended predominantly by bishops from this region and from North Africa, often with only token representation from the Western (Latin) Church. The Councils were also convened by the incumbent secular or political rulers of the time, who frequently took an active part in the debates.

It is not altogether surprising that the Churches in the East do not regard the Fourth Council of Constantinople as a valid Ecumenical Council and on the death of Patriarch Ignatius in AD 887 (i.e. the Western Church's candidate), they unilaterally reinstated the earlier patriarch, Photius, as a purposeful gesture of defiance against Rome. This was another event in what had become an increasing state of friction between 'the two sides' concerning a range of ecclesial issues and which, in 1054, culminated in a formal split or 'schism'. This division was accompanied by the serving of reciprocal excommunications by Rome and Constantinople.

And so the first millennium of Christianity ended with what is known as the 'Great Schism', in which the Churches of the East and West ceased to be in brotherly communion with each other and set off on their separate ways. Sadly, it is a situation that is still unresolved almost a thousand years later.

So much for the call by Jesus for all of us to be one (Jn 12:17) (1 Cor 10–12).

COUNCILS OF THE MIDDLE AGES

The immediate consequence of the Great Schism was that attendance at Councils could no longer be automatically assumed to include bishops from 'the whole of the known world', and raised the question of whether or not future Councils could continue to be referred to as ecumenical? The view of the Eastern Churches (which we generally refer to today as 'Orthodox Churches') was 'no', whereas the Roman Catholic Church continued to apply this designation when referring to Councils that were considered to involve issues of importance for the whole of the Christian community. However, there has been a tendency of late for Catholic authorities to refer to Councils after 1054 as 'General Councils' and sometimes even 'General Councils of the West'.

From this time onwards it would be the Popes rather than civic or political leaders who would be the principal instigators of Councils and a decision to call a General Council today is the sole prerogative of the incumbent Pope. All General Councils following the Great Schism have also been held in locations in Western Europe.

The First Lateran Council (1122)

The Council was convened by Pope Callistus II and held at the Lateran Palace in Rome. Its principal purpose was to establish the autonomy of the Church; to ensure that the election of bishops and abbots was free from secular influences; to re-establish the principle that spiritual authority emanates from the Church; and to abolish claims of the Emperors to be able to exercise their influence in papal elections.

The Pope attended the Council in person together with 300 bishops and 600 abbots, and as well as dealing with matters concerned with the independence of the Church, they examined a range of issues relating to marriage (to include the issue of consanguinity) and expressed opposition to marriage and concubinage among priests, deacons, monks and nuns.

Their deliberations also extended to the subject of 'simony', namely the trafficking of ecclesiastical offices, roles and spiritual pardons for money. In particular, to end the practice of ecclesiastical benefices being conferred by lay people in which property and income is provided in respect of pastoral duties.

The Second Lateran Council (1139)

Following the death of Pope Honorius in 1130, a further schism developed within the Western Church involving two competing Popes: Anacletus II and Innocent II. Following the death of the former in 1138, Pope Innocent II convened a Council in order to formally ratify his position, and to draw up measures to strengthen ecclesiastical morals and discipline, which he considered to have become progressively lax.

The agreed provisions included a formal endorsement of the rule of celibacy for clerics from the subdiaconate onwards and provided for the removal from office of clerics who had obtained a benefice by means of a financial transaction. The Council also sought to enforce the so-termed 'Truce of God', which was a peacekeeping initiative that involved the prohibition of feuding (endemic in society at the time) and violence of any kind taking place within specifically designated geographical locations. It also barred a Christian burial for anyone who had participated in any jousts or tournaments that endangered lives.

The Third Lateran Council (1179)

This was a Council to formally confirm the ending of what had been yet another schism. This particular incident was the result of a long-standing dispute between Pope Alexander III and a series of antipopes who had been promoted by the German Emperor Frederick Barbarossa as part of his political ambitions in respect of Italy.

In addition to confirming the status of Pope Alexander III, the Council decreed that any future candidate for the papacy must receive a two-thirds vote of the cardinals, reconfirmed the requirement for a bishop to be unmarried, and stipulated that to become a bishop the candidate must be at least thirty years old. It also issued a formal condemnation of a 'heresy' (i.e. a deviation from formally and publicly pronounced teaching of the Church), which was being promoted by a movement in the South of France known as 'The Cathars' or 'Albigensians'.

Their deviation was along similar lines to the earlier mentioned Gnostic belief of an unending dualistic struggle between the principles of 'good' and 'evil'; a proposition that they took to reject anything related to the flesh. It was a philosophy that had previously been condemned by the Church as antithetical to the belief in one God who had created all things and the Council reiterated the Church's traditional opposition to cremation, as a means of emphasising a reverence for the human body that forms part of the body of Christ and is a temple of the Holy Spirit.

The Fourth Lateran Council (1215)

It might be said that the first three Lateran Councils could in some way justify the title 'ecumenical', albeit that they were not concerned with matters as fundamental as the Trinitarian and Christological Councils of the earlier centuries. As for the Fourth Lateran Council, this was both planned and convened to be an Ecumenical Council by Pope Innocent III, who invited his fellow bishops:

> '…to attend in accord with the practice of the ancient Fathers… to eradicate vices and to plant virtues, to correct faults and to reform morals, to remove heresies and to strengthen faith, to settle discords and to establish peace, to get rid of oppression and to foster liberty, to induce princes and Christian people to come to the aid and succour of the Holy Land.'[6]

This is a formidable agenda by any standard and it was accompanied by a pre-prepared schedule of answers for more than seventy individual provisions that Innocent III and his Curia (his Rome-based bureaucracy) considered to be the most important aspects of dogmatic and moral theology for the universal Church. These included a further rebuttal of the 'Cathar' heresy;

---

[6] Referred to by Norman Tanner, *The Councils of the Church: A Short History* (Crossroad Publishing, 2001), p52.

the necessity of Church membership for salvation; the declaration of seven sacraments in the life of the Church to include a first mention of 'transubstantiation' in respect of the Eucharist; a requirement for the faithful to go to confession and receive Holy Communion at least once a year. It also listed a number of proposals in order to reform abuses relating to relics. One disturbing provision that appeared within a list of behavioural and disciplinary measures was a requirement for Jews to wear distinctive clothing at all times and to stay off the streets during Holy Week each year.

The Council was attended by over 400 bishops, patriarchs from Constantinople and Jerusalem, envoys representing the patriarchs of Antioch and Alexandria, abbots and priors as well as a number of representatives of secular powers. As the list of individual provisions and disciplinary measures had already received prior papal approval, Innocent simply called for and received an automatic endorsement by the attending bishops.

As a footnote to this Council, Pope Innocent III died less than a year later, which had the effect of lessening what might otherwise have been the momentum to follow through and establish the ecclesial framework that had been envisaged in his original declared propositions. There then followed a series of disruptive political events such as the Mongols entering Eastern Europe (1241), the fall of Jerusalem to Islam (1244), the Greeks threatening the Latin Empire of

Constantinople, and the German Emperor, Frederick II, threatening the papacy's political power in Italy.

The Council of Lyons (1245)

When the German Emperor Frederick II attempted to capture Pope Innocent IV (1243–54), he fled to his home city of Genoa, but being unable to organise a Council in Italy, he moved to Lyons and invited his fellow bishops to join him there. The Council of Lyons opened in June 1245, ostensibly to deal with the above threat and to consider possible additional reforms pertaining to the clergy. However, this turned out to be a blatantly political Council, which resulted in the disposition of Frederick II as King of Germany and the Holy Roman Empire, but with little else to show in resolving the various other ecclesial problems that had been listed for attention.

The Church's concern for the Crusader States persisted for the rest of the 13th century and during this time there were twelve successive papacies. This included a unique papal election following the death of Pope Clement IV in 1268 when the cardinals spent three years wrangling over his successor, which eventually resulted in the civic authorities removing the roof of the palace where the conclave was taking place and threatening to starve the cardinals until they reached a decision. They did eventually elect the

Archdeacon of Liege – who, as it happened, was on a crusade at the time – but on his return to Europe, he was consecrated in 1272 as Pope Gregory X.

The Second Council of Lyons (1274)

Not surprisingly, the welfare of the Crusader States was one of the main agenda items for Gregory X and prompted him to call a further Council in Lyons, which opened in May 1274. This allowed him the opportunity to convince the 200 or so bishops in attendance to surrender a percentage of their annual revenue in order to support the ongoing Crusader cause.

In addition to the bishops, Gregory invited the Emperor of Constantinople, the King and Primate of Armenia and the Great Khan of the Mongols, who was rumoured to be sympathetic to Christianity. He also invited several Greek envoys in an attempt to achieve a reunion between the Eastern and Western Churches. In the event, a reunion did not materialise and neither did the conversion of the Mongols. The only real achievement was a reform of the papal election procedure to prevent a repetition of the earlier deadlock at future papal conclaves.

The Second Council of Lyons is sometimes included in history's list of 'what ifs'. This is because Gregory's intention had been to employ the best theological talent that he could find at that time in order to expand upon and develop aspects of Church teaching. His choice of experts included the Dominican Friar, Thomas Aquinas, but sadly St Thomas Aquinas, as he is now officially recognised, died en route to the Council, leaving open the question of what might have been the outcome had he attended?

The Council of Vienne (1311)

With the fall of Acre as the last Christian possession in the Middle East, papal attention turned towards Europe and the potential challenges to the papacy's political power resulting from the emergence of a growing number of Nation States. High on the list of potential protagonists was King Philip IV of France, and in 1305, a Frenchman was elected to the Papacy, who, as Clement V, chose to move from Rome to a papal estate in Avignon in Southern France.

King Philip needed money to finance his wars and decided to expropriate the funds of the Knights Templar, a religious order founded to protect pilgrims to the Holy Land and which had become wealthy and powerful as a result. The Templars were accused of introducing perverse and diabolical practices and the Pope was urged to condemn and disband them on religious grounds. Clement was afraid to take this step alone and so he called a Council that would take place in the French town of Vienne.

This is a Council that has to be judged as scandalous. Clement invited only a purposely selected group of bishops to attend and the King's agents dominated the proceedings to ensure that the Templars were found guilty and suppressed in order for their assets to be seized.

The next seven Popes continued to reside in Avignon until 1377, when Pope Gregory XI returned to Rome, thus ending seventy-two years of Avignon Papacy.

The Council of Constance (1414)

Gregory XI died within a year of his return to Rome and the Roman populace demanded that the next Pope should be a Roman, or at least an Italian, to ensure that there would be no return to Avignon. Their wishes were granted with the election of Pope Urban VI in 1378.

However, it was not long before Urban VI became generally unpopular and was considered by the cardinal electors to be a potential threat to their individual safety. This prompted them to flee from Rome and to declare that they had only voted to elect him because they were under pressure to do so and that his election was therefore invalid. They then proceeded to elect a new Pope, who took the name Clement VII, and both he and the cardinals returned to Avignon.

The secular rulers across Europe were divided in their respective allegiances to the two 'acting' Popes.

They sought to resolve the situation by calling a Council at Pisa in 1409, but this only managed to produce a third Pope as the two earlier 'appointees' refused to resign. The Church's scholars and canonists concluded that only an Ecumenical Council could end what was now another Church schism, and led by the German Emperor Sigmund, the bishops met in the Swiss City of Constance in 1414.

The first item on the Council agenda was 'Conciliarism'. This was a subject that had been under discussion for some time in seeking to determine whether supreme power in the Church should be held by the Pope or by an Ecumenical Council. On this occasion, the motion in favour of authority residing in an Ecumenical Council secured the support of a majority of the bishops and was set down in two formally approved Council Decrees. The first of these titled '*Sacrosancta*' confirmed the decision in favour of a General Council holding supreme authority in the Church and the second, '*Frequens*', mandated that such Councils should take place on a known regular basis.

As regards *Sacrosancta,* the finally agreed text was as follows:

> 'In the name of the holy and undivided Trinity, Father, Son and Holy Spirit. Amen. This holy synod of Constance, which is a General Council for the eradication of the present schism and for bringing

unity and reform to God's Church in head and members, legitimately assembled in the Holy Spirit to the praise of almighty God, ordains, defines, decrees, discerns and declares as follows in order that this union and reform of God's Church may be obtained the more easily, securely, fruitfully and freely.

First, that legitimately assembled in the Holy Spirit, constituting a general Council and representing the Catholic Church militant, it has power immediately from Christ; and that everyone of whatever state or dignity, even papal, is bound to obey it in those matters which pertain to the faith, the eradication of the said schism and the general reform of the said Church of God in head and members.

[…] Anyone of whatever condition, state or dignity, even papal who contumaciously refuses to obey the past or future mandates, statutes, ordinances or precepts of the sacred Council or of any other legitimately assembled General Council regarding the aforesaid things or matters pertaining to them, shall be subjected to well-deserved penance, unless he repents, and shall be duly punished, even by having recourse, if necessary, to other support of the law.'[7]

---

[7] Ibid, p66.

As regards the accompanying Decree, *Freequens,* this proposed that:

> 'the frequency of general councils is a pre-eminent means of cultivating the Lord's patrimony. It roots out the briars, thorns and thistles of heresies, errors and schisms, corrects deviations, reforms what is deformed and produces a richly fertile crop for the Lord's vineyard. Neglect of Councils, on the other hand, spreads and fosters the aforesaid evils. This conclusion is brought before our eyes by the memory of past times and reflection on the present situation.
>
> For this reason we establish, enact and ordain by a perpetual edict, that general councils shall be held henceforth in the following way. The first in five years immediately after the end of this council, the second in seven years immediately after the end of the next council and thereafter to be held every ten years for ever... Thus by a certain continuity, there will always be either a council in existence or one expected within a given time.'[8]

Having formally resolved these provisions, the bishops then proceeded to elect Pope Martin V, who was the candidate found to be acceptable to virtually all

---

8 Ibid, p67.

of those in attendance. They then addressed an alleged heretical teaching of a religious teacher from Eastern Europe called Jan Hus who had been summoned to attend in order to explain his views. Despite a guarantee of safe passage, the bishops reneged on their promise and Hus was declared guilty of heresy and executed.

The Council of Basle (1431)

In accordance with the Decree *Frequens*, which had been approved at the Council of Constance, Pope Martin V (1417–1431) called for a Council to be held in Pavia in 1423, but because of the plague it was earmarked for a transfer and then suspended. Pope Martin did eventually call for a further Council, which began in Basle in 1431, but he died a few weeks later.

Attendance at Basle was poor and Pope Martin's successor, Pope Eugene IV, decided to dissolve the Council but the bishops who were already in attendance invoked *Sacrosancta*, which had been approved at Constance and refused to be dissolved. They also voted to assume direct responsibility for running the daily affairs of the Church.

On the horizon at that time was a further possibility of a reunion between the Eastern and Western Churches and a tentative meeting had been proposed by the Byzantine Emperor in the hope of securing support from the Church in the West against the threats being posed by the Turks. In order to facilitate such a meeting, Pope Eugene IV suggested that the Basle Council should transfer to Ferrara in Italy but a large number of bishops refused to leave Basle, thereby creating a further schism – this time involving two competing Councils. By 1439, the Basle Council had deposed Eugene and elected Pope Felix V – so the Church could now boast of having two competing Popes as well as two competing Councils.

These two Councils continued in parallel, with the Ferrara contingent moving first to Florence in 1439 and then to Rome where it concluded in 1445. An agreement was reached for the Eastern and Western Churches to reunite, but this only lasted until the Eastern delegates returned home and their respective local Churches collectively declared a preference for 'the turban rather than the tiara'. A wish that was fulfilled in 1453 with the fall of Constantinople.

Meanwhile, the Basle contingent transferred itself to Lausanne in 1443, becoming progressively smaller and more disorganised, and in 1449 Pope Felix V resigned. The Church could therefore return to having only one Pope, who by this time was Nicholas V, who had been elected by the Ferrara contingent in 1447. This was an outcome that was declared to be a victory for the papal cause because it had come about without any formal instigation, endorsement or approval by a General Council.

The problem that remained for the papacy was how to reconcile the decisions reached and recorded at Constance confirming that supreme authority in the Church was in the hands of a formally convened Ecumenical Council. The argument presented by the papacy was that the declarations relating to Conciliarism were taken when there were two papal candidates in contention and therefore it was a decision that could not be judged as either valid or binding. Moreover, as the eventually agreed new Pope Martin had not been asked to give formal consent to the concept of Conciliarism at the time of his election, this was considered to add further strength to the argument that this had been an invalid proposition and would always remain so.

The Fifth Lateran Council (1512–17)

The Council marked a return to the Lateran Palace after a break of almost 300 years, and it was called by Pope Julius II in order to settle a further period of wrangling concerning ultimate authority in the Church. The Council reaffirmed the earlier decision in favour of the papacy and then proceeded to approve a 'Concordat' (an agreement between the Church and a secular Government) with France to cover matters of mutual concern to both parties.

The bishops also passed a number of reform decrees, but conveniently ignored some of the worst abuses, and the proceedings were eventually brought to a conclusion on grounds that there were no further issues of contention that warranted their continued attendance. Seven months later, an altogether different approach to reform began in Germany, led by the Augustinian Monk, Martin Luther, and signalled the start of the Protestant Reformation. This was a movement that would eventually result in almost one third of the population of Catholic Europe departing from Roman obedience.

COUNCILS FOLLOWING THE REFORMATION

Following the death of Pope Julius II in 1513, his three immediate successors continued to adopt a 'business as normal' approach in Rome despite the increasing level of turmoil across Europe as a result of the Reformation. It was not until the election of Pope Paul III in 1534 that any real consideration was given by Rome to introduce possible countermeasures. The Pope concluded that the only effective remedy to contain and reverse the situation created by the Reformers was to call a General Council, but fearing that this might reignite the previous interest and support for Conciliarism, he put off making a final decision for a further eleven years.

The Council of Trent (1545–63)

Pope Paul's Council eventually began in 1545 in the

Northern Italian town of Trent, by which time more than twenty-eight years had passed since Martin Luther had nailed his *Ninety-Five Theses* to the door of the Castle Cathedral in Wittenberg. The ensuing Council would comprise three intermittent working sessions spanning a total of seventeen years, with an agenda that included a number of doctrinal considerations, as well as a long overdue list of reform measures covering a broad range of ecclesial practices.

The first working session of Trent ran from 1545 to 1547 and dealt immediately with the topic of 'authority' – in the sense of what is the determining source for Christian belief. One of the principal claims of the Reformers was that belief is based purely on the Scriptures (*Scritura solo*), whereas the Catholic view was that the living Tradition that had developed around the Scriptures should also be taken into account. That in addition to the written word, it is appropriate to have regard to the manner in which the apostles responded to and implemented the verbal instructions they were given by Jesus and which they, in turn, bequeathed to their successors in title under the guidance of the Holy Spirit.[9]

A further assertion by the Reformers concerned 'justification', namely what was necessary for a person to achieve salvation? Their contention was that

---

9   Ibid, p79.

salvation could be possible through faith alone (*fidei solo*) as opposed to the Catholic belief that it should be a combination of faith and good works. This was an issue that touched upon the concept of 'original sin' and the continuing presence of God's grace, which, by its very nature, was considered by the Catholic Church to call for an active and positive response from each individual. This was a response that was made possible as a result of the seven Sacraments of the Church, which had been defined and declared as such at the Fourth Lateran Council and were strongly reiterated by the bishops at Trent.

There was then an outbreak of the plague at Trent, which forced the session to be suspended. Its resumption did not commence until 1551, by which time the Church had come under the authority of Pope Julius III. Invitations were sent to a number of the Reformers who indicated a willingness to attend, but on condition that the earlier agreed principle of Conciliarism would be acknowledged and upheld. This was a demand that the Catholic bishops were unwilling to accept and when news then broke that there was a Protestant army advancing in the direction of Trent, a number of the bishops departed and the remainder declared in favour of suspending the proceedings.

Pope Julius III was succeeded by Pope Paul IV in 1555, but he refused to recall the Council. This had to wait for his successor, Pope Pius IV, who reconvened a further working session in 1562. This final session at Trent concluded with numerous approved decrees to include a definition of the Mass as a sacrifice, a strengthening of the doctrine of transubstantiation, the calling of provincial synods, and the establishment of seminaries for the training of priests. When the Council was formally brought to a close in 1563, it had firmly restated Catholic doctrine and dealt with many of the original abuses cited by the Reformers, but in taking almost forty-six years to reach this position, a 'new order' had already become well established throughout Europe.

The Council of Trent did nevertheless represent a turning point for the Church by fulfilling the wishes of many Catholics for genuine and sustainable reforms to a range of anomalies in Church practices and it provided the Church with the necessary theological ingredients for what would become known as 'the Counter-Reformation'. As history would later attest, the 'robust' manner in which individual provisions were drafted at Trent resulted in many of these being treated as wholly definitive and unquestionable Church Dogma for the next 400 years.

This was a period that witnessed significant changes in society and in people's outlook in general. The discovery of new continents, the emergence of democratic nation states, industrialisation and urbanisation all contributed to a different order and scale of priorities that were no longer instigated and orchestrated by the Church. The *Christianitas* of medieval Europe – the partnership between Church and state (and generally understood in that order!) – no longer carried sway and the eventual loss of control over Papal States in Italy to the Nationalist forces caused some people to question whether future Popes would be able to continue to govern the Church.

In the intellectual sphere, the 18th century saw the emergence of 'the Enlightenment' or the 'Age of Reason', whose proponents introduced the idea of religious toleration but downgraded religious belief, tradition and authority, and emphasised reason as the path to truth and human well-being. Significant advances were made in the sciences, to include an improved understanding of the composition and the workings of our physical universe, and the 'Theory of Evolution' as a means to explain our emergence as a species.

These were topics that had previously been thought of as exclusively Church territory, and in response to what was considered to be society's increasingly secular (even anti-Catholic) aims, the Church became progressively introspective and defensive. In 1864, Pope Pius IX issued a *Syllabus of Errors,* which comprised the wholesale condemnation of a wide range of contemporary theses. It served to supplement an earlier papal *Index* of books that were considered dangerous for the faithful (including theologians) to read and were banned under threat of excommunication.

In the field of theology, the standard Church curriculum at the time of Trent was based on the teaching of St Thomas Aquinas. Unfortunately, the way in which some of Aquinas's work had become interpreted did not always accurately express his original intentions and this, too, became a contributory factor in the process of estrangement between the Church and the emerging trends of thought in society.

An example of this was the understanding of the relationship between 'nature' and 'grace' – that as a result of a belief that humankind is created in the image and likeness of God, we each possess an inbuilt orientation or desire that directs us beyond the purely finite aspects of our lives. As this had been described by St Ireneaus (died: AD 202), 'The glory of God is man alive and the life of man is the vision of God.' Years later, St Augustine (died: AD 430) expressed this as, 'You have made us for yourself (Lord) and our heart is restless until it rests in you.'

The way in which this was described by St Thomas Aquinas was that every intellect naturally desires the vision of the divine substance, but later theologians drove a wedge between his use of the two components of 'natural' and 'divine', such that natural desire became assumed to exist only for things with a natural end, and a further intervention by God was necessary to implant a desire for things divine or supernatural.

This may seem to represent a minor point of difference but the theory of 'pure nature', which developed out of this change in perspective, has created serious repercussions. In the words of Paul McPartlan, the Church traditionally had something to say to everybody because it knew the same natural desire was always seeking its higher fulfilment, but with this desire no longer being thought of as an 'intrinsic component' of human nature, Christianity found itself with little to say to those who happily claimed to be able to do without it, or who had not yet received the requisite additional and supernatural call from God. Philosophy and theology moved from being open to one another to being closed realms that could travel their different ways. Philosophy could proceed on its own without any account of religion.[10]

The First Vatican Council (1869)

It was against this background that Pope Pius IX (1846–1878) decided to convene a further Council even though the decrees and formulations from the Council of Trent were still judged by many in the Church to provide a comprehensive exposition of

---

10   Referred to by Paul McPartlan, *The Sacrament of Salvation: An Introduction to Eucharistic Ecclesiology* (T&T Clarke, 1995), p51.

Catholic theology. Nevertheless, the Council began in St Peter's Basilica in 1869 in the presence of 800 cardinals, patriarchs, archbishops, bishops and heads of male religious orders.

In his formal summons to the bishops for them to attend the Council (known as a 'Papal Bull'), Pius's stated objective was:

> 'to provide a remedy for present evils in the Church and society; to determine what is to be done in these calamitous times for the greater glory of God, for the integrity of belief, the splendour of worship, the eternal salvation of humanity, the discipline and the solid instruction of the secular and religious clergy, the observance of ecclesiastical laws, the reform of morals, the Christian education of youth and peace and universal accord.'[11]

Invitations to attend were sent to the Orthodox Churches and the more recent Reformation Churches but these were expressed in terms of providing an opportunity [for them], to return to 'the true faith'. Not altogether surprisingly, there were no positive responses.

A total of fifty-two draft documents had been prepared for discussion, but only six of these actually

---

11   Referred to in *The Modern Catholic Encyclopedia* (Dublin: Gill & Macmillan, 1994), p887.

managed to reach the Council floor. And, as a result of external political and military circumstances, the bishops only had time to debate two of these discussion papers:

1. The Catholic Faith (*Dei Filius*: Son of God)
   This dealt with God as the Creator of all things; Revelation; the nature of faith itself; and the interconnection between faith and reason. The aim of the document has been described as being to seek to steer a middle course for the Church between the excessive exaltation of the 'authority of reason' exemplified by the Enlightenment and an 'automatic' in-principle rejection of reason as a characteristic of prevailing religious fundamentalism.[12]

2. The Constitution on the Church of Christ (*Pastor Aeternus*)
   The original intention had been to define the primacy of the Pope, but this was later expanded to include the concept of Papal Infallibility. Whilst Infallibility had been a subject of discussion in some Church circles, it had not been specifically listed as an agenda item in the original Papal Bull.

In the event, *Pastor Aeternus* defined both Papal Primacy

---

12 Norman Tanner, *The Councils of the Church: A Short History* (Crossroad Publishing, 2001), p88.

and Papal Infallibility and was approved by the bishops with only two noted dissents. The actual document comprised four chapters, which covered: the institution of the primacy of the Pope; its continuation; its extent; and a definition of Papal Infallibility.

The concept of a primacy being due to the Pope as the Bishop of Rome and successor to the title of St Peter was not new nor, in itself, an issue for most Catholics or indeed some other Churches. What did become a matter of concern was the wording of the eventual definition that the Pope had:

> '...full authority not only in matters of faith and morals but also in those which concern the discipline and government of the Church dispersed throughout the world... an absolute fullness of this supreme power... ordinary and immediate over all and each of the churches and over all and each of the pastors and faithful.'[13]

As this has been described subsequently by Bishop Geoffrey Robinson, it was a definition that separated the Pope from the body of bishops, and rather than serving them, they could now be seen to serve him. The notion of the Pope as 'the principle of unity' became a notion of the Pope as 'the principal of direction'. The

---

13   Ibid, p90.

universal Church could become treated as the Pope's own diocese, and the original idea of the diocese of Rome possessing primacy because it was the place where St Peter gave witness to his calling vanished in favour of the idea of a Pope possessing a personal primacy because of the words of Jesus to be found in the Gospel of St Matthew – 'Thou art Peter and on this rock I will build my Church' (Mat 16:18).[14]

The original intention was for *Pastor Aeternus* to be a composite document that would cover all aspects of the Church, but the external issue mentioned previously was the imminent arrival in Rome of Nationalist military forces and caused the bishops to abruptly adjourn the proceedings. As a result, they only had time to discuss the papacy in isolation instead of this forming one component within the intended broader framework of the Church as a whole.

As regards the Decree on Papal Infallibility, the formally agreed pronouncement stated:

> '…therefore, faithfully adhering to the tradition received from the beginning of the Christian faith, to the glory of God our Saviour, for the exaltation of the Catholic religion and for the salvation of the Christian people with the approval of the sacred council, we teach and define as a divinely revealed dogma that

---

14 Geoffrey Robinson, *Confronting Power and Sex in the Catholic Church* (The Columba Press, 2007), p116.

when the Roman Pontiff speaks *ex-cathedra,* that is when, in the exercise of his office as shepherd and teacher of all Christians in virtue of his supreme apostolic authority, he defines a doctrine concerning faith or morals to be held by the whole Church, he possesses by the divine assistance promised to him by blessed Peter, that infallibility which the divine Redeemer willed his Church to enjoy in defining doctrine concerning faith and morals. Therefore, such definitions of the Roman Pontiff are of themselves and not by the consent of the church, irreformable.'[15]

There are several points within this definition that need to be properly understood. The Pope has to be speaking in solemn form, *ex-cathedra* (symbolically, his chair of office), and his infallibility must be understood as being part of the Spirit-led infallibility that Jesus intended to be enjoyed by the whole Church – not something different, outside or in addition to it. The Pope here needs to be understood as acting as the representative of the Church, not of God.

Moreover, infallibility is only engaged where there is a question of defining doctrine and to 'define' is a precise term in this context. It does not cover teaching in general, or preaching or theological expositions. It is simply and solely the making of a formal and limiting

---

[15] Referred to by Norman Tanner, *The Councils of the Church: A Short History* (Crossroad Publishing, 2001), p91.

judgement in order to clarify the understanding of an existing facet within the Church's recognised 'deposit of faith'.[16]

In practice, and even with this explanation, it is easy to see how the doctrine identifies the Church with the Papacy, so that expressions such as 'the Church says' or 'the Church teaches' are often understood as meaning 'the Pope says' or 'the Pope teaches' and with the Bishop of Rome becoming treated less as the bond of unity and charity in the Church and more as an oracular figure to be revered in his person with quasi-sacramental fervour.[17] This is not to question the office of the Pope but rather the tendency to presume that every statement that emanates from Rome represents a definitive and irreformable statement – sometimes referred to as 'creeping infallibility'.

The first Vatican Council with its formally approved teaching on Papal Primacy and Papal Infallibility would therefore seem to mark the end of centuries of arguments concerning ultimate authority in the Church. The irony, of course, is that the reason why Papal Primacy and Papal Infallibility are now acknowledged and accepted is because it was a Council that declared them to be so!

As for the Council itself, the proceedings were suspended, and this remains its official status.

---

16   Ibid, p92.
17   Gabriel Daley, 'Faith and Theology' in *The Tablet*, April 1981, p391-2.

Shortly after the suspension, Pope Leo XIII (1878–1903) issued an Encyclical (a formal Papal letter) titled *Rerum Novarum*, which sought to defend the rights of workers in the face of the prevailing social and political conditions of the times. However, support within the Church for this form of papal involvement was by no means universal and subsequent Popes who attempted to exert some influence in the social sphere or to broker peace settlements between protagonists met with limited success. In the words of Ronald Musto, 'The modern state was at best indifferent to Christian goals and at worst nakedly hostile to them.'[18]

In the decades that were to follow the First Vatican Council, we were forced to endure two World Wars, adjust to major changes in political, economic and social mores, and come to terms with unprecedented advances in the sciences. The principal 'enemy' of the Church over this period became seen as 'Modernism', which was a movement that had grown out of the Enlightenment and was judged to be a philosophy that sought to eliminate God from all social life by questioning the nature of the scriptures and traditional thought in relation to God, to humankind and even to doubt any particular purpose for life itself. It became a requirement for each candidate for the Catholic priesthood to sign an 'anti-modernism oath' as a precondition for their ordination.

---

18   Ronald G. Musto, *The Catholic Peace Tradition* (Orbis Books, 1986), p174.

By the middle of the 20th century, the Church was led by Pope Pius XII (1939–58), whose pontificate was generally regarded to have been a steadying influence during World War II and the period of political and social upheaval that followed. He provided a similar level of assurance for many people within the Church with his adherence to traditional Catholic teaching in the face of changing social patterns and the growing array of new worldly philosophies and accompanying movements.

One of the criticisms of Pius XII was the rigidity in the way official Church teaching was presented, which gave rise to what became termed a 'separated theology'. A theology where all encounters between faith and the world outside were assigned to apologetics – a wholly defensive method of approach in which faith can become the end product of ever more numerous and ever more remote arguments. It was no longer seen primarily as the means through which to attempt to achieve a better understanding of reality.[19]

The tendency of the Church's leadership to become inward-looking and isolationist in approach was accompanied by a whole raft of rigid ecclesial provisions intended to ensure complete doctrinal compliance. As described by the historian and theologian Joseph

---

19 Referred to by Joseph Komonchak, 'Theology and Culture at Mid-Century: The Example of Henri de Lubac in *Theological Studies*, Vol. 51, Issue 4, 1990, p582.

Komonchak, the Church's theology came under the closest supervision and tightest control by the authorities that theologians had ever experienced and it was a discipline that was taken seriously only, or at least chiefly, within a Catholic subculture.[20]

This all said, it was possible to present a highly positive overview of the Church at this mid-point of the 20th century. The Catholic population was continuing to grow and was estimated to represent over 17 per cent of the total world population at that time, with almost half of its membership living in countries outside Europe. The Church itself was served by some three thousand bishops who were assisted by close to 500,000 ordained priests. The various Congregations and Religious Orders could be seen to be thriving and most seminaries of students training for the priesthood were full. The Church looked to be in overall 'good shape' and there were no apparent major heresies in prospect.

The Second Vatican Council (1962-65)

Pope Pius XII died on 9th October 1958 and on 28th October 1958, Cardinal Angelo Roncalli from Venice was elected as his successor. This was a surprise selection because the new Pope was not part of the Rome 'inner

---

20 Ibid, p579.

circle', having spent most of his ordained life as a Vatican envoy in overseas postings, and he was already seventy-eight years old.

A further surprise was the new Pope's choice of name, which he announced as John XXIII – the same as a previously discredited Pope from the 15th century, and behavioural surprises were set to continue with Pope John in contrast to the more austere and measured approach of his predecessor. As examples, he was asked soon after his election how many people worked for him in the Vatican, to which his immediate response was 'about half of them'. And, in the run up to Christmas that year, he announced his intention to visit the inmates in the Regina Coeli prison in Rome on grounds that as they were unable to travel and wish him a happy Christmas, it was up to him to visit them.

The major surprise from Pope John occurred at the end of January 1959 during the closing ceremony for that year's week of prayer for Christian Unity, which took place in the Basilica of St Paul Outside the Walls. This was the announcement of his intention to convene a synod for the priests of the diocese of Rome and a General Council for the Universal Church.

The decision to call a General Council was totally unexpected even by the members of the Curia. After all, it was less than a hundred years since the last Council and a widely held view in the Church was that the now formally declared 'infallible Pope' and his trusted Curia could surely be relied upon to handle all future contingencies without the assistance of another Council.

In contrast, Pope John intuited that there was something out of synch in the inner life of the Church; intellectually sterile, liturgically lifeless; moral instructions depending more upon imperatives than initiatives; fear emphasised over hope; a clergy cut off from the laity; the razor wire of the Reformation still dividing Christianity; the living word of Scripture all but forgotten; Jesus himself on the margin of piety.[21] A sobering list of concerns but arguably a 'checklist', which might usefully warrant being revisited from time to time.

What was not widely known in the Church at this time was the behind-the-scenes struggle that had been taking place between those seeking to preserve the status quo and those wishing to explore a broader understanding of the Church's essential mandate and its relationship with the rest of the world. With the benefit of modern scholarship, a number of theologians had reopened studies on the Bible, the origins and development of the liturgy, the insights and the teachings of the early Church Fathers, as well as the whole subject of 'ecumenism' in the sense of unity (or the lack of it) between different beliefs.

---

21   James Carroll in Norman Tanner, ed., *Vatican II: The Essential Texts* (NY: Crown Publishing, 2012), p17.

These theological groups or movements were referred to in some quarters as *Nouvelle Theologie* (new theology), which was intended as a derogatory title in that they were accused of attempting to introduce new ideas and concepts into established Church teaching. In reality, this was the exact opposite of what these movements were attempting to achieve, which was to re-examine and better understand the teachings and practices of the early Church as the source of the 'Great Tradition' – the process whereby truths become handed on from generation to generation. These several movements would eventually find their natural expression in Pope John's Council.

The preparatory work to set up and organise the Council took more than two years to complete. This began with the appointment of an 'Ante-Preparatory Commission' whose task was to gather opinions from the bishops and others about issues needing action. The results of this consultation provided the material that was then sifted, organised and formulated into texts to be presented to the Council at its inauguration.

The Council was formally opened by Pope John in St Peter's Basilica on 11th October 1962. Present at the opening ceremony were more than 2,400 of the Church's bishops, together with representatives from other Christian denominations. In his opening address, Pope John outlined four principal themes to shape the course of the Council: a celebration of the faith, ever old, ever new; an optimism in the Spirit to dispel the prophets of doom; a clear statement of what the Council was for; and a novel approach to errors.[22]

For Pope John, authentic doctrine was to be studied and expressed in light of modern research methods and in the language of modern thought. In his words, 'The substance of an ancient deposit of faith is one thing and the way in which it is presented is another.'[23] And as a departure from what had been the traditional practice for Councils to formally censure dissenting opinions and other deemed errors, he went on to state that, 'Today the Spouse of Christ (the Church) prefers to use the medicine of mercy rather than severity. She considers that she meets the needs of the present age by showing the validity of her teaching rather than condemnation.'[24]

This was a clear signal that Pope John intended Vatican II to be a pastoral event. His reference to dispelling prophets of doom was directed towards the not insignificant number of his fellow bishops who regarded their principal role as simply being to preserve all present teachings and practices without change in order to protect the Church from what was viewed to be a hostile secular world that had lost its way and all sense of values.

---

22   Referred to by Tony Castle, *Good Pope John and his Council* (Kevin Mayhew Publishers, 2006), p41.
23   Ibid, p43.
24   Ibid, p44.

The planned programme for the Council was for the bishops to attend a working session of around ten weeks in St Peter's Basilica in order to debate and vote upon a series of proposals (schema) that had been tabled for their consideration. The Council would then adjourn for several months to allow the bishops to return to their respective dioceses and during this time a standing committee would edit and circulate all of the relevant paperwork with a view to obtaining a further response from each bishop. The results from this additional consultation would then be used to prepare an agenda for the next working session.

There were some suggestions that Vatican II should represent a continuation of the previously suspended Vatican I, but this was clearly not the intention of Pope John. A number of the bishops also considered that essential Council business could be dealt with in a single session, but as events transpired it took four working sessions to achieve this, which ran between October 1962 and December 1965.

The first working session
(12th October 1962–8th December 1962)
The season of surprises was not over. The initial item on the agenda was the assumed formality of approving a list of named bishops who would operate the various Council Commissions, together with their accompanying theological experts (*periti*). The list of

appointments had been compiled and circulated by the Curia but was not to the liking of a large number of the bishops who sought and successfully secured an immediate adjournment to allow them time to consider alternative nominations. Thus, the inaugural working session of Vatican II lasted less than thirty minutes and, as one commentator described it, 'The bishops streamed out of the Basilica into the autumn sun, having regained control of their council.'[25]

For those of us who were alive at the time, the opening of the Council was widely covered by the media and in one UK newspaper I remember seeing a centre-page photograph of the bishops in the nave of St Peter's Basilica under the headline, 'Never again in your lifetime will you witness a scene like this'. It was a time that will also be remembered for what became known as the 'Cuban Missile Crisis' with the threat of an all-out nuclear war between the United States of America and the Soviet Union. Happily, war was averted and the bishops were allowed to continue with their deliberations, which, for the first time in history, would take place under the live gaze of the world's media. It was not long before differences of opinion between the bishops started to become evident and developed into a topic in its own right.

Attendance throughout the first session continued to average around 2,400 bishops out of a total of some

---

25 Ibid, p44.

2,900 invitees. A number of bishops were too old or too infirm to attend and the majority of bishops whose dioceses were in Communist countries had been refused permission to travel.

It was to be expected that an assembly of this size (described in one publication as the largest ever meeting in the history of the world) would need time to 'find its feet' in terms of its internal workings and procedures. The previously mentioned motion for an adjournment on the subject of nominations was soon followed by calls for the withdrawal and substitution of an entire draft document that had been earmarked to deal with the relationship between Scripture and tradition.

The first working session was therefore viewed by some observers as a lean period in terms of productivity as no documents were finally agreed. However, a first draft for the intended Constitution on the Liturgy was approved and discussions had at least begun on other subjects such as the nature of the Church, Church Unity and the media.

The second working session
(29th September 1963–4th December 1963)
During the recess between the first and second sessions, the various commissions worked to complete their task of updating earlier drafts in line with the pastoral needs of the Church as Pope John had outlined in his opening

address. It was also decided to limit the scope of the Council discussions to matters of more general interest, leaving detailed items and issues considered to be of lesser moment to a series of commissions that would be established after the Council and which would be charged with responsibility to handle the 'small print', and to deal with adjustments or new insertions to the Church's Code of Canon Law.

Sadly, Pope John died on 3rd June 1963 whilst the Council was in adjournment. Tributes were forthcoming from around the world and included messages from many individuals and organisations that had not previously been particularly well disposed towards the Catholic Church. This was a measure of the impact and genuine affection which 'Good Pope John' had generated during his comparatively short forty-eight-month papacy.

By 21st June 1963, the cardinals had elected his successor, who took the name Paul VI and who, in his first radio address the following day, announced (to the relief of the majority of bishop delegates), 'The main duty of our pontificate will be the continuation of the Second Vatican Council.' It needs to be remembered that in modern times it is the sole prerogative of the incumbent Pope to sanction the calling or the continuation of a General Council.

Pope Paul soon became energetically involved in producing and issuing revised regulations concerned with the running of the Council, and correcting procedural and organisational defects that had become apparent during the first working session. In terms of actual Council business, he opened the second working session with an address in which he asked the Council to set out its understanding of (i) the nature of the Church and the role of bishops, (ii) renewing the Church, (iii) restoring Christian Unity and (iv) initiating a dialogue with the modern world.

During the course of this second working session, the bishops finally approved the 'Constitution on the Sacred Liturgy' (*Sacrosanctum Concilium*), which was formally promulgated (made known by public declaration) by Pope Paul on 4th December 1963. So, too, was a 'Decree on the Mass Media' (*Inter Mirifica*) and discussions continued on documents concerned with the nature of the Church, bishops and ecumenism.

The third working session
(14th September 1964–21st November 1964)
The high point of this session was the promulgation of three further agreed documents, which took place on 21st November 1964. These were 'The Dogmatic Constitution on the Church' (*Lumen Gentium*); 'The Decree on the Catholic Eastern Churches' (*Orientalium Ecclesiarium*); and 'The Decree on Ecumenism'(*Unitatis Redintegratia*).

By way of explanation, the accompanying Latin

titles are the way in which official Church documents are referred to. This is to name them by using the opening few Latin words as they appear in the document.

Aside from these three agreed documents, discussions continued on all other outstanding agenda items, but Pope Paul expressly excluded two topics for him alone to consider. These were clerical celibacy and the Church's existing prohibition of artificial means of birth control, for which he appointed a special commission to study and report to him directly.

The fourth working session
(14th September–8th December 1965)
This final session saw the promulgation of eleven further documents: 'The Decree on the Pastoral Office of Bishops in the Church' (*Christus Dominus*); 'The Decree on the Training of Priests' (*Optatum Totius*); 'The Declaration on the Relation of the Church to non-Christian Religions' (*Nostra Aetate*); 'The Dogmatic Constitution on Divine Revelation' (*Dei Verbum*); 'The Decree on the Apostolate of Lay People' (*Apostolicam Actuositatem*): 'The Declaration on Religious Liberty' (*Dignitatis Hunanae*); 'The Decree on the Church's Missionary Activity' (*Ad Gentes Divinitus*); 'The Decree on the Ministry and Life of Priests' (*Optatum Totius*); and 'The Pastoral Constitution on the Church in the Modern World' (*Gaudium et Spes*).

The Documents of the Council

As above, the bishops secured Papal consent for a total of sixteen documents. These comprised Four Constitutions, Nine Decrees and Three Declarations.

The difference between a constitution and a decree can be said to spring from the different levels of strata found in Christian teaching. For example, beliefs concerned with the nature of Jesus and the place of the Trinity in God's plan are fundamental and will normally be dealt with in a constitution. Other beliefs like the relationship between bishops and priests are obviously important but they could be dealt with by a decree.

Both constitutions and decrees can contain elements that contribute towards the development of Church Teaching, namely the ongoing process of improving our understanding of the message and example of Jesus. Declarations are generally intended simply to cast light on existing laws and matters of Church Governance.

For present purposes, I propose to concentrate on the four approved constitutions.

The Constitution on the Sacred Liturgy: Sacrosanctum Concilium (SC)

This was the first document to be discussed and agreed at the Council, which no doubt reflects the importance the bishops attributed to the liturgy (public worship) in the life of the Church. The document identifies five guiding principles: to protect the rich patrimony of the Church; to offer guidelines for reform; to base itself on Church Doctrine; to inspire the clergy with a deeper 'liturgical spirit'; to promote a more active participation by the faithful.

The approved constitution begins by stating that the liturgy 'through which the work of our redemption takes place, especially in the divine sacrifice of the Eucharist, is supremely effective in enabling the faithful to express in their lives and portray to others the mystery and the nature of the true Church' (SC #2). The liturgy is described as an exercise of the priestly office of Jesus Christ, from which it follows that every liturgical celebration is an action of Christ the priest and his body the Church and is therefore a pre-eminently sacred action that exceeds all others (SC #7). The liturgy is seen as 'the summit toward which the activity of the Church is directed; it is also the source from which all its power flows' (SC #10).

In order for the liturgy to achieve its full effect, the pastors of souls are called upon to realise that their obligations go further than simply ensuring that the laws governing valid and lawful celebrations are observed. They are required to ensure that the faithful take part fully aware of what they are doing, actively engaged in the rite and enriched by it (SC #11). Taking an active part in liturgical celebrations is therefore demanded by the very nature of the liturgy and Christian people have a right to do so by virtue of their baptism, which makes them 'a chosen race, a royal priesthood, a holy nation, a redeemed people' (SC #14).

Prior to the Council, the prayers at Mass were either spoken in Latin or recited silently by the priest who for most of the time stood with his back to the congregation. The laity were merely required to be present without any active participation. *Sacrosanctum Concilium* sought to change this by emphasising that the laity 'should not be at Mass as strangers or as silent spectators but should be encouraged to actively and devoutly take part in the sacred action' (SC #48).

To this end, the Council Fathers proposed that the Mass should be simplified by eliminating duplications that had occurred over time and reinstating other elements that were lost through the vicissitudes of history, but with due care being taken in all cases to preserve its essential substance (SC #50). This included giving greater attention to Bible readings (SC #51), a re-introduction of prayers by the faithful – i.e. bidding prayers (SC #52), and for Holy Communion under both kinds to be permitted in agreed circumstances (SC #55).

Acknowledging the cultural diversity that exists within the Church, *Sacrosanctum Concilium* was anxious not to impose rigid liturgical uniformity, but rather to attempt to cultivate and foster the qualities and talents of different races in matters not affecting the underlying faith and well-being of the entire community. Anything in people's way of life that is not bound up with superstition and error would be studied by the Church with sympathy and, if possible, be retained (SC #37). Subject to prior approval by the Apostolic See, bishops in individual territories were given leave to admit adaptations to their liturgy that they considered to be useful or necessary having regard to prevailing cultural and educational conditions (SC #40).

Contrary to popular belief, Vatican II called for Latin to be preserved (SC #36) and for care to be taken to ensure that the faithful are able to say and sing together in Latin, those parts of the liturgy that pertain to them (SC #54). Nevertheless, it was acknowledged that there were circumstances when it could be advantageous to use the vernacular and scope should be given for this to be introduced (SC #36). In practice, the use of the vernacular soon became the norm although individual language translations would remain subject to the jurisdiction of a Congregation of Divine Worship, which was one of Pope Paul VI's promised commissions to oversee the implementation of approved liturgical provisions.

I believe it fair to say that for most people who lived through the Council years, Vatican II will be remembered mainly (if not solely) for the changes introduced to the Mass. One explanation for this, which is offered by Oxford Emeritus Professor Maurice Wiles, is that people do not usually feel deeply over matters of faith or statements of doctrine unless they are considered to bear upon the exercise of their piety. Any variations to the way in which Mass is conducted could therefore be expected to touch on sensitivities of this nature.

I find it disappointing that a number of the liturgical changes indicated by the Council continue to be a source of contention within the Church. I regard this as an issue that has been poorly handled by our pastoral leadership in not providing an adequate explanation at the time of why changes were proposed, the nature and background to the changes themselves and the whole approach subsequently concerning the intended use (or non-use) of Latin. Despite such explanations being encouraged by *Sacrosanctum Concilium,* I cannot recollect a coordinated programme of this kind ever being provided at parish level.

A new Roman missal (Latin and English) was approved for general use by Pope Paul VI in 1970, which, by coincidence, happened to be the 400th anniversary of an earlier missal introduced by Pope Pius V following the Council of Trent. The original Pius V missal contained a prohibition against any form of change, and I imagine that many people in the Church may still consider this to be a binding provision and are supporters of the view that a Latin Mass and, in particular, the 'Tridentine Latin Mass' represents the peak of 'liturgical maturity'.

The Dogmatic Constitution on Divine Revelation: Dei Verbum (DV)

The approved document begins by declaring that its purpose is: 'to set forth authentic teaching on divine revelation and its transmission, for the whole world to hear the summons to salvation, so that through hearing it may believe, through belief it may hope and through hope it may come to love' (DV #1).

The document sought to expand upon the earlier text from the Council of Trent by linking scripture and tradition more closely together. An initial draft was rejected by the bishops on grounds of being seen to treat scripture as being literally accurate in all respects and for viewing tradition as if it was a separate and almost independent source of revelation. The actual wording of the draft was also considered to be negative, rigid and too quick to condemn when viewed in the context of the pastoral and ecumenical objectives set by Pope John.

The debate that followed can be said to be a reflection of the underlying issue that the Council had been called to examine, namely the intended purpose of the Church. Are we meant to be a wholly autonomous authority that is charged with responsibility for maintaining a perpetual state of vigilance and defence of established doctrinal purity against ever-emerging new errors, or are we a community passing through history and attempting to hand on the Good News we received from Jesus as best we can through our Spirit-gifted approach to life, worship and teaching?

It was the latter viewpoint that eventually secured the support of the bishops to determine the outcome of this particular debate, but a final agreement on the wording for *Dei Verbum* was not reached until November 1965. This declared that:

> 'By divine revelation God wished to manifest and communicate both Himself and the eternal decrees of His will concerning the salvation of humankind, and as the first principle and the last end of all things He can be known with certainty from the created world by the natural light of human reason' (DV #6).

The document went on to confirm that sacred tradition and sacred scripture should not be considered as two distinct sources, but as two streams that spring from the one divine well spring, which communicate with one another and merge and flow towards the same goal.

'Sacred scripture is the utterance of God put down in writing under the inspiration of the Spirit, and tradition transmits in its entirety the word of God which has been entrusted to the apostles by Christ the Lord and the Spirit; it transmits it to the successors of the apostles so that, enlightened by the Spirit of Truth, they may faithfully preserve, expound and disseminate it by their preaching' (DV #9).

The task of giving an authentic interpretation of the word of God, whether in its written form or in the form of tradition, is entrusted to the living teaching office of the Church to be exercised in the name of Jesus Christ. This 'magisterium' (teaching authority) is not superior to the word of God but is rather its servant. It teaches only what has been handed to it. At the divine command and with the help of the Holy Spirit, it listens to this devoutly, guards it reverently and expounds it faithfully. All that it proposes for belief as being divinely revealed, it draws from this sole deposit of faith (DV #10).

Acknowledging that sacred scripture is God speaking through human beings in a human fashion, *Dei Verbum* urges the interpreters of the written word to ascertain what God wished to communicate to us by carefully searching out the meaning that the sacred writers really had in mind by paying due attention to literary genres (DV #12). In other words, whilst the scriptures are a product of the Spirit working in the minds of the authors, we should avail ourselves of all of the modern techniques in biblical research to determine the relevant historical foundations (historical criticism), the known verbal proclamations (form criticism) and the dominant ideas at the time that governed the writing and editing (redaction criticism).

The Dogmatic Constitution on the Church: Lumen Gentium (LG)

This is the cornerstone document of the Council in seeking to meet the declared aims of its two presiding Popes. For Pope John, this was *aggiornamento* – to bring the Church up to date or, to use his frequently reported expression, 'to open the windows and let in some fresh air'. For Pope Paul, it was *ressourcement* – to revisit the message of Jesus as it had been received and experienced in the infant Church.

In this way, *Lumen Gentium* can be said to have concluded the work begun at the Council of Trent by expressing our understanding and appreciation of what it means to be Catholic. The finally agreed document comprises eight chapters.

Chapter One: The Mystery of the Church
The opening sequence declares that:

'Christ is the light of the nations and consequently this holy synod, gathered together in the holy Spirit, ardently desires to bring to all humanity that light of Christ which is resplendent on the face of the church, by proclaiming his Gospel to every creature' [see Mk 16:15.], (LG #1).

First and foremost, therefore, the Church acknowledges its existence as being purely a means of presenting Jesus to the world. It describes itself as a 'sacrament' – a sign and instrument of communion with God and the unity of the entire human race, so that '...by communicating his Spirit, Christ mystically constitutes as his body his sisters and brothers from every nation' (LG #7).

We begin then to understand the Church as something that is alive within each of us, not simply an organisation but rather an organism of the Holy Spirit that is constantly sustained here on earth as a community of faith, hope and charity. We are the body of Christ. He is the head and we are the members and through this visible society and spiritual community, Christ communicates truth and grace to everyone (LG #8).

This is the unique Church of Christ, which we profess as being 'one, holy, catholic and apostolic'. However, as a marked departure from earlier claims of exclusivity, *Lumen Gentium* states that: the Church which is constituted and organised as a society in the present world 'subsists in' the Catholic Church which is governed by the successor of Peter and by bishops in communion with him' (LG #8). The expression 'subsists in' as opposed to 'is' the Catholic Church is an acknowledgement that elements of sanctification and truth can be found outside the Church's visible confines and serves to dispel the often heard missive that there is no salvation outside the Catholic Church.

As for the Church itself, it is seen to require human resources to carry out its mission, but this is not in order to seek earthly glory. Rather, it is to proclaim its objectives in humility and to encompass with its love all those who are afflicted by human infirmity, and to recognise in those who are poor and who suffer the likeness of its poor and suffering founder (LG #8).

Chapter Two: The People of God
The emphasis here is the unity of baptismal hope, which is held by all members of the church without distinction. It is a concept that can be traced back to the *Old Testament*, which describes the ongoing unity of God's involvement with a particular people and gives shape to the idea of the Church being a new Israel, a pilgrim people, made up of Jews and Gentiles and which would be one – not according to the flesh but in the Spirit. As a pilgrim people, we are seen to be continually on the move towards our final

destination and always in need of renewal along the way (LG #9).

The chapter goes on to introduce a broader constituency for the 'people of God' in order to consider the relatedness of the Catholic Church to other Christian affiliations as well as to non-Christians (LG #15/16). Our specific mandate is to pray and work so that '...the fullness of the whole world may move into the people of God, the body of the Lord and the temple of the holy Spirit and that in Christ, the head of all things, all honour and glory may be rendered to the Creator, the Father of the universe' (LG #17).

Chapter Three: The Church is Hierarchical
The first two chapters define the Church as a work of God, a means of his presence in the world and at the same time a community of people who are called together to be 'one in the Spirit'. Then, and only then, is there any mention of an intended structure and a hierarchy to assist in the carrying out of this collective responsibility. The ordering here is deliberate, not random.

The Gospels record that Jesus appointed a group of twelve disciples with Peter as lead spokesperson in order to represent a lasting and visible source of unity in both faith and communion. In like fashion, *Lumen Gentium* provides that the Roman Pontiff as Peter's successor in title and the bishops as heirs to the title of the apostles should continue to undertake this combined service to the people of God through their collective association (LG #21).

The appointment of the original twelve signified a community that existed in the communal union of the group, whereby each individual had significance not in his own right, but because of being in union with the others. In the early Church, bishops were responsible for their 'local Churches', but were also conscious of a collective or collegial responsibility for the wider Church, and this same understanding of 'collegiality' in the service of the Universal Church is reaffirmed by *Lumen Gentium* (LG #22).

Chapter Four: The Laity
The term laity refers to all of the faithful who are not in Holy Orders or belong to a religious congregation, but who, through baptism, become sharers in the priestly, the prophetic and the kingly office of Christ. Their vocation is stated to be the building-up of the Church with a specific brief to engage in temporal affairs and to direct them according to God's will (LG #31).

The apostolate of the laity is therefore a sharing in the Church's saving mission and as such it constitutes a specific theological component. The laity are not simply to be thought of or treated as the general public or as customers, or simply clientele, and they are entitled – and sometimes duty-bound – to express their opinion on matters that concern the good of the Church (LG #37).

This all said, I find it somewhat disappointing that the role of the laity is linked specifically to the secular sphere as, by implication, this could suggest that the ordained are to be engaged in a separate and exclusively spiritual realm. I regard this as an example of a lingering tendency towards dualism in the Christian thought process (remember *Gnosticism*?), which places one thing against another: the spiritual and the temporal, the sacred and the profane and, despite our common baptism, the clergy and the laity.

Chapter Five: The Universal Call to Holiness
Everyone in the Church is called to the holiness of life that Jesus initiated and brings to perfection for each of his disciples, no matter what their condition of life:

> 'For he sent the Holy Spirit to move them interiorly to love God with their whole heart, with their whole soul, with their whole understanding and with their whole strength and to love one another as Christ loved them… They must therefore hold on to and perfect in their lives that holiness which they have received from God' (LG #40).

Holiness is an attempt to come closer to God and remain so, and we are encouraged to use the strength that each of us has been given by the life and example of Jesus to move steadfastly along the way of a living faith in whatever state and way of life we pursue. This is a faith that arouses hope and operates through love (LG #41).

Chapter Six: Religious
Being a 'Religious' is described as a life in its own right, not some middle way between priest and laity. Those who embrace this way of life bind themselves to the three evangelical counsels of poverty, obedience and chastity by vows or other sacred ties (LG #44). The Religious withdraw from the world, but do not cut themselves off from the faithful and instead give witness to the transcendence of heavenly goods by dedicating themselves to the service of God and of their neighbour.

Chapter Seven: The Pilgrim Church
The Church in which we seek to attain holiness by God's grace will receive its perfection only in the glory of Heaven (LG #48). It was the specific request of Pope John that the Council should say something about the saints, as in his view '…the doctrine of the Church would be mutilated if this part of the Church, which is already united to Christ but still intimately united with the pilgrim Church on Earth, was not included.'

It is in the liturgy that our union with the heavenly Church is best realised. It is here where we cherish the memory and example of those who have gone before us and by the practice of fraternal charity, the union of the whole Church in the Spirit is strengthened. This is the 'Communion of Saints', which we profess in our weekly *Credo* (LG #50).

Chapter Eight: Our Lady
Mary is rightly held as a pre-eminent member of the Church; she is its template and outstanding model in faith and charity (LG #53). She is seen not merely as a passive instrument, but as freely cooperating in the work of human salvation through faith and obedience (LG #56).

Mary cares for her son's sisters and brothers who still journey on earth and is invoked under the titles of advocate, helper, benefactor and 'mediatrix'. But as *Lumen Gentium* makes clear, these titles do nothing to diminish or add to the dignity and efficacy of Jesus as our 'One Mediator' (LG #52).

The underlying constant that can be seen to link all eight chapters of *Lumen Gentium* is that the Church is essentially a 'Eucharistic Community'. It came into existence at Jesus's last supper with his apostles when they received the feast of life and it continues in our own time when we, the body, come together with Jesus as our head, in order to celebrate the re-enactment of his death and resurrection.

The Eucharist – the supreme act of thanksgiving – enjoins men and women to each other and to Jesus and in this way turns us into being the Church. As this was memorably expressed by Henri de Lubac, one of the *periti* at Vatican II, 'The Eucharist makes the Church'.

It is in this way that the Church's liturgy brings together a diversity of outlooks and personalities that would not otherwise occur, and whenever and wherever we meet as a community, Jesus gives himself complete and undivided. As this is described by *Lumen Gentium,* each legitimate local community is itself a manifestation of the Church. Jesus is fully present in each community, as it is in and from them that the one true and unique Catholic Church exists as a 'communion of communions' (LG #23).

In terms of the interface between each local Church and the universal Church, this is stated to reside in the bishops who are called to facilitate the offering of the one unifying Eucharist with the faithful who are in their direct charge. It is through the Eucharist that the relationship between the Roman Pontiff and the bishops throughout the world forms a collegiate community, living in communion with one another in a bond of unity, charity and peace (LG #22).

These are insights that, in my view, combine to make Vatican II 'radical' in the true sense of the word; namely, to point us back to our roots in order to rediscover and understand concepts and practices as they were originally understood and experienced by the apostles. By revealing these to be genuine components of our long Catholic tradition, *Lumen Gentium* is able to lay to rest a number of the more recent and questionable claims of what constitutes the Church and governs the way in which we are expected to function.

The unmistakeable message of *Lumen Gentium* is that the Church is the great Pascal Sacrament where the risen Jesus encounters us in the community of the Spirit and continues to sustain us as a community as we travel together in seeking to extend his offer to the world at large. To see the Church only as an organisation is not to fully understand what is intended. The Church is a living thing and our relationship to it must also be life.

The Pastoral Constitution on the Church in the Modern World: Gaudium et Spes (GS)

This was not on the original list of *schemas* that had been circulated prior to the Council. It was a topic that had been prompted by Pope John, but the decision to introduce it did not take place until the Council proceedings had begun and the revised team of Coordinators had been appointed. Credit for its successful introduction is generally accorded to Cardinal Leon-Joseph Suenens from Belgium.

I consider that the opening paragraph of *Gaudium et Spes* warrants being quoted in full:

'The joys, the hopes, the grief and the anguish of the people of our time and especially those who are poor or afflicted, are the joys and hopes, the grief and the anguish of the followers of Christ as well. Nothing that is genuinely human fails to find an echo in their hearts. For theirs is a community of people united to Christ and guided by the Holy Spirit in pilgrimage towards the Father's Kingdom, bearers of a message of salvation for all of humanity. That is why they cherish a feeling of deep solidarity with the human race and its history' (GS #1).

In this statement, the Church formally signalled its intention to re-engage with the world and to indicate its willingness to enter into a dialogue with the whole of humanity in order to, 'throw the light of the Gospel on the various issues, difficulties and concerns that humankind is facing, and for this to be a two-way exercise of mutual interaction (GS #3), adopting a language that is intelligible to each generation' (GS #4). There is even a willingness to acknowledge how richly the Church had profited by the history and development of humanity (GS #44).

Gaudium et Spes is the longest of the Council documents and is arranged in two parts. Part One examines the present state of affairs in the world under several headings, which include: 'the dignity of the human person', 'the community of humankind', 'work and human activity' and 'the Church's own role in the modern world'. As examples, the dignity of the human person is stated to rest firmly on the belief that humankind has been created in the image and likeness of God, which makes it all the more lamentable that there are people who are unaware of this vital link. It also raises the question in passing of whether the Church might in some way be responsible for this state of affairs?

As regards the human community, we are encouraged to treat each other with mutual respect as true neighbours, not simply co-components or mere statistics in an increasingly technological environment (GS #23). We are called to focus on the common good – the sum total of social conditions to allow people to reach their fulfilment more fully and more easily – and the resultant rights and obligations this entails (GS #26). And for us to recognise, in addition, that we are only stewards of the material goods we possess (GS #30).

The autonomy of humanity and of organisations involved in the discovery, utilisation and ordering of the laws and values of matter and society are also fully acknowledged provided they do not override moral laws or conflict with them (GS #36). In this regard, the traditional Catholic view of conscience is elaborately reaffirmed:

> 'Deep within their conscience men and women discover a law which they have not laid upon

themselves and which they must obey. Its voice ever calling them to love and do what is good and to avoid what is evil, tells them inwardly at the right moment; do this, shun that. For they have in their hearts a law inscribed by God. Their dignity rests in observing this law and by it they will be judged. Their conscience is people's most secret core, and their sanctuary. It is there that they are alone with God whose voice echoes in their depths' (GS #16).

In terms of the Church's role, this is stated as being to exhort Christians to faithfully perform all of their earthly duties and to do so always in the spirit of the Gospels. To strike a balance between disregarding current affairs and responsibilities because of a sole focus on our future destiny or immersing ourselves in earthly affairs to such an extent that religion becomes seen as nothing more than fulfilling occasional acts of worship and the observance of a few moral obligations. To avoid what is described as 'the pernicious opposition' between professional and social activity on the one hand and religious life on the other (GS #43).

Part Two of *Gaudium et Spes* looks at topics such as marriage and the family, the proper development of culture, the political community, freedom and the peace of nations. In terms of marriage, the notion of 'responsible parenthood' enters the Catholic vocabulary with married couples being told to be ruled by their conscience albeit with the reminder that this should be in accord with the teaching authority of the Church (GS #50). There is an obvious element of ambiguity here resulting in considerable soul-searching among married couples that continued until the 1968 Papal Encyclical, *Humanae Vitae*, which restated the Church's traditional opposition to all forms of artificial birth control. This is a subject that continues to be an issue of serious contention and to which many of the faithful no longer subscribe.

A further topic of immediate concern at the time was the whole question of war and peace between nations. Recalling the possibility of a nuclear war, *Gaudium et Spes* contains the strongest condemnation (it is, in fact, the only outright condemnation in any of the documents) against the total destruction of cities or other extensively populated areas. Effectively, this relates to the use of nuclear weapons, which it describes as 'a crime against God' (GS #81).

As a formal Church document, *Gaudium et Spes* was the first to have been addressed to the whole of humanity and not just its own faithful, and the final voting at 2,307 in favour with only seventy-five against is an indication of how far attitudes can be said to have changed within the hierarchy since Vatican I in terms of an apparent willingness to participate with others. The role of the Church was seen as being 'not only to communicate divine life to humanity, but to cast the reflective light of the divine over all of the Earth, notably in the way it heals and elevates the dignity of the human person, in the way it consolidates society and endows people's daily activity with a deeper sense of meaning'(GS #40). It was the firm belief of the Council Fathers that through the activities of its members and its community as a whole, the Church could help to make the human family and its history more human.

Prior to bringing the Council to a close, Pope Paul announced his intention to establish a regular programme of 'bishop's synods', which would report to him in a consultative capacity. He also announced the creation of a number of commissions that would be responsible for implementing approved Council provisions. And finally, as a gesture of ecumenism, he met Patriarch Athenagoras I, as a representative of the Orthodox Churches, and both prelates formally withdrew the mutual excommunications imposed by their predecessors in 1054.

And so, three years and two months after its opening ceremony, Vatican II was closed by Pope Paul VI on 8th December 1965 – the feast day of the Immaculate Conception of Mary and which, on this occasion, was accompanied by a Papal announcement that Mary would henceforth be described as 'Mother of the Church'. In his closing address, Pope Paul declared that all Catholics were bound by the Council's decisions and all actions undertaken knowingly or through ignorance against such teachings were invalid. Bishops were also urged to resolve all items of unfinished business, as well as continuing to search for pastoral solutions that are responsive to the underlying needs of the times. In his words, '*aggiornamento* should mean for us an enlightened insight into the Council's spirit and a faithful application of the norms which it has set forth in such a felicitous and holy manner.'[26]

In my view, Vatican II provided us with an enlightened explanation of what constitutes the Church and the way in which we can and should be working in concert to achieve what Jesus asked us to do. This involves not simply 'keeping the faith' but 'proclaiming the faith' beyond existing Church boundaries, and by engaging in world affairs and causes that serve to promote the common good of humanity and our shared environment.

The Post-Vatican II Church

Despite the level of voting in favour of each of the Council Documents, there were reports of lingering differences of opinion among the bishops on various issues, which for ease of reference were categorised by the media under the broad banners of 'Conservative' and 'Progressive'. The former was applied to those

---

[26] Referred to by Ormond Rush, *Still Interpreting Vatican II* (Paulist Press, 2004), pix.

who were considered to be supportive of the deemed certainties of beliefs, practices and accompanying rigid governance structures that were in place prior to the Council, with the latter for those who were seen to favour an opportunity to explore and develop the Church's doctrine and liturgy within a less constricted environment.

I believe it fair to say that in the period immediately following the close of Vatican II, the 'progressive wing' was in the ascendancy and, depending upon one's viewpoint, most details that began to emerge were treated as either the new standard or the scapegoat by which to explain everything that was happening in the Church. As this was described by another of the Council's *periti*, Yves Congar:

> 'There was a simplistic practice of applying the pattern "before" and "after" to the Council as though it marked an absolute new beginning, the point of departure for a completely new Church which loses the continuity of tradition. Vatican II was one moment; and neither the first or the last moment in that tradition – just as Vatican I, the Council of Trent and the Councils of history were neither the first nor the last.'[27]

---

27 Yves Congar, 'A Last Look at the Council' in Alberic Stacpoole, ed., *Vatican II by those who were there* (London: Geoffrey Chapman, 1986), p351.

On this same topic, the then Fr Joseph Ratzinger (the late Emeritus Pope Benedict XVI) stated that, in his view, the Council did nothing but reaffirm the continuity of Catholicism. There were no leaps in this history, no fractures or break in continuity and '… in no wise did the Council intend to introduce a temporal dichotomy in the Church.'[28]

It is a truism that the perfect religious organisation with the divine and the human in total harmony has never existed and never will. An element of tension can be a positive factor in our collective vocation, but it is the behaviour of the individual parties that will determine if or when this starts to become counterproductive. Sadly, the verbal and literary exchanges between the conservative and progressive factions in this initial period were often condemnatory and sometimes acrimonious.

The situation was further exacerbated with the publication of Pope Paul's Encyclical, *Humanae Vitae*, in 1968, which reconfirmed the Church's opposition to any artificial form of birth control. In anticipation of a different judgement, many Catholics had already begun to use contraceptives and few of these expressed a willingness to return to 'authorised' practices. It is not possible to say what individual pastoral advice was sought or given, but there was evidence of some priests

---

28   Ormond Rush, *Still Interpreting Vatican II* (Paulist Press, 2004), p6.

being suspended for being unwilling to emphasise the Papal ruling in their weekly homilies.

An official statement eventually emerged from Rome to confirm that *Humanae Vitae* was not an infallible teaching, but this was judged to be of doubtful benefit. For many couples, *Humanae Vitae* was the catalyst for them to cease further active involvement in the Church and there is little doubt that this document represents a watershed in people's attitude towards Church authority in general. It should be recorded that Pope Paul did not produce another Encyclical during the remainder of his pontificate, preferring instead to issue advisory letters.

A further post-conciliar statement of note came from Abbot Christopher Butler, who had been present at Vatican II as a representative of the English Benedictine Order. His original prediction at the close of the Council was that it would take at least thirty to forty years for its message to be fully implemented, but he later increased his time frame to 130 years, on grounds that he saw little evidence in Rome or among his fellow bishops of an enthusiasm to fully promote the teachings of Vatican II.[29]

As events have transpired, Abbot (subsequently 'Bishop') Butler's assessment looks to have been prophetic and we continue to witness the same 'pyramid-

---

29 Referred to by Tony Castle, *Good Pope John and his Council* (Kevin Mayhew Publishers, 2006), p8.

style' approach to Church governance as it was before the Council. At the apex is the Pope, beneath him his Curia, beneath them the bishops and their respective priests, with the laity occupying the remainder of the space at the base of the pyramid. The presumption is that the Holy Spirit communicates with the Church via the apex and directives are then allowed to filter down as considered necessary or appropriate. Very much the centralised, proscriptive and authoritative model that Vatican II had sought to modify by emphasising the Church as the People of God, and for authority to be understood as service in the buildin-up of God's kingdom on Earth.

With the benefit of hindsight, I consider that we were ill-prepared for Vatican II. Most of us at the time had little knowledge of what an Ecumenical Council involved or what we might expect from it. The Church was as we had always known it to be and which has been described as having 'its peace, its certainties, its clarities, its regimentations and its carefully forged chain of command'.[30] Was this capable of being improved?

Vatican II introduced us to a much broader vision of what should be our individual and collective vocation, but we were provided with limited practical information and assistance to help us to fully understand what was being proposed and why changes

---

30   Gabriel Daley, 'Faith and Theology' in *The Tablet*, April 1981.

were considered necessary. It is also surprising that a Church with such a hitherto distinctive and disciplined set of characteristics seemed to have been prepared to allow itself to almost drift into a new *modus operandi* without a coordinated and supportive official input to help manage the process.

As described by the late Emeritus Pope Benedict XVI, 'Whilst the Council formulated its pronouncement with the fullness of the power that resides in it, its historical significance will be determined by the process of classification and elimination that takes place subsequently in the life of the Church. In this way, the whole Church participates in the Council; it does not come to an end in the assembly of bishops.'[31]

What is being described here is 'the reception' of a Council, namely the action of understanding, interpretation and application, whereby basic texts enter or are assimilated into the conscious practice of the Church. As the statement makes clear, it is a process which is intended to involve the whole of the Church, and which incorporates different roles and functions as well as drawing upon different perspectives of race, culture, geography and local history.

It seems evident some sixty years later that the reception of Vatican II is still very much a case of a 'work in progress', but with little evidence of any continuing

---
31   Referred to by Ormond Rush, *Still Interpreting Vatican II* (Paulist Press, 2006), p53.

and wholehearted support from our pastoral leadership. In my view, this is a disappointing result so far to what I regard as being the genuine promptings of the Spirit in our own times.

PART TWO

WHAT TO BELIEVE?

I grew up in a happy family environment with loving Irish parents. This made it easy for me to visualise a loving 'Father' in heaven who had created all the good things around us and who counted each of us as His children. All that was required in return was to show our gratitude by the way in which we lived our lives and, in particular, by the manner in which we treated other people.

My starting point was therefore the faith story imparted by my parents and their continuing witness to this belief, which provided me with first-hand experience of being loved and an enduring sense of what it means to belong. It was an upbringing I now appreciate as a perfect foundation at the time and an ideal stepping stone for later life.

In due course, I was introduced to the Bible with its story of God's act of creation, its description of the first misdemeanour committed by humankind and the ongoing trials, tribulations, hopes and joys of a people whose behaviour was sometimes open to question but who were never abandoned by God. The high point in the story was the decision by God to take on a human presence in the person of Jesus of Nazareth, who would thereafter be our role model to the extent of being willing to suffer and to die for his efforts.

The next item in my religious learning process was what was commonly referred to in those days as the *Penny Catechism*.[32] This was a small booklet comprising 370 individual questions and answers, which were intended to amplify what Jesus had said and done, how we should respond to his teachings and a list of the things in life that we should strive to avoid.

The Church of my childhood was therefore well structured and documented, with the key features of being Catholic in those days being 'Certainty', 'Conformity' and 'Community'. Behavioural decisions were, for the most part, dictated by our pastoral leadership and their instructions were generally delivered with an assurance of authenticity and an expectation of compliance. Teachings were presented as a statement of fact without elaborate explanations and were often expressed in absolute terms to leave no doubt what was considered to be right or wrong, sacred or profane, true or false, good or bad.

---

32 *A Catechism of Christian Doctrine* (Catholic Truth Society, latest ed 1997). Affectionately known as the *Penny Catechism* because of its one-time price.

A combination of certainty and conformity could, of course, give rise to what has been termed 'Clockwork Catholicism'[33], of being wound up as children like clockwork toys in order to continue to observe and perform a range of ritual observances in a purely mechanical fashion. This would accompany us into adulthood as an outward observance of the stated rules and regulations of religion, but without necessarily generating an informed and responsive inner conviction.

For some people, the rigidity of the arguments in support of what was forcefully presented as 'The One True Faith' eventually reached a breaking point and they ceased to remain actively involved. For others, it is quite possible that their adult understanding of fundamental beliefs still dates back to their school-day catechism, with minimum subsequent enhancement. Faith by 'rote' has long been a feature of Church life, but this can no longer be relied upon in the same way in today's more questioning environment.

This is certainly the reality with younger Catholics, who are generally less willing than earlier generations to simply accept propositions at face value and especially if these include claims of absolute uniqueness. They require teachings to be explained in terms of their underlying value and purpose in order for them to judge

---

33 Christopher Lightbound, *The Church Then and Now* (St Pauls, 2004), p29.

the relevance to their own everyday life experiences. The continuing fall in the number of active younger Catholics is a good indicator of where catechetical attention needs to be directed.

Catechesis itself can be described as the process of transmitting the Gospel of Jesus as the Christian community has received it, understands it, celebrates it, lives it and communicates it. It is an ever-evolving process of discernment as opposed to being a fixed point of reference, as whilst the essential message of Jesus is unchangeable, our understanding of its import will continue to develop and expand and always needs to be expressed in a manner suited to prevailing circumstances.

This was certainly understood in the early Church where decisions became superseded through a process of thought and prayer, of giving way to more scholarly prudence, or if something that was hidden became known. I am not convinced that this policy is applied to the same degree in the Church today, where the emphasis by those in a position of authority seems to be directed more towards preserving the *status quo*, as if we are already in possession of the definitive text of God's plan for creation and have answers for all conceivable questions that may arise from this.

We live in an information-driven society with access to almost unlimited data at the touch of a button. It is an interactive environment that allows, and indeed promotes, the idea of greater direct participation by each person, and this has produced a marked change in the way we tend to think and act, as well as how we expect to be treated.

In terms of the Church, the original *Penny Catechism* with its question-and-answer format is still in print and can now be accessed online. In addition, we have a more expansive summary of beliefs (2,836 individual entries!), which are contained in the *Catechism of the Catholic Church* (published in 1994). By today's standards, I would regard the former publication as rather light on detail whereas the latter could be judged to represent the opposite extreme for a majority of potential readers.

In my view, our pastoral leadership needs to recognise the knowledge gap that exits between biblical and theological scholarship and current levels of popular faith. They should attempt also to improve the way in which they express the essentials of the faith to include the use of a vocabulary that more closely matches the currents of modern thought. An excessively dogmatic approach is no longer conducive either to strengthening the faith of those who have one or to successfully introducing the concept to those who do not.

One of the few benefits of the recent lockdowns during the Covid-19 pandemic was the time it afforded to reflect on the general state and direction of one's faith journey. An opportunity to review how much of what one was taught as a child continues to ring true today, and how best to try and interpret present authorised Church teaching in light of one's outlook and experiences as an adult. I found this to be a reassuring exercise in many respects, but a cause for disappointment and concern in others.

My principal disappointment is that the sense of enthusiasm for religious issues generated at the time of Vatican II seems to have all but evaporated and there are still a number of insights that continue to be overlooked or ignored. My concern is the way in which the Church continues to conduct itself both internally and externally and the resultant adverse impact on the credibility of our essential message.

We need to realise that there is no longer an automatic constituency for the Christian message and that we are in competition with other persuasive and well-funded concepts in an environment in which 'relativism' has become a social grace. We are frequently viewed as an introspective organisation with self-interest high on our agenda; an entity that claims to hold all of the answers, which expects to receive total membership conformity and which displays a noticeable dislike of modernity in any form.

Not the ideal starting point for us to promote Jesus in our 21st-century world.

GOD AND CREATION

At its simplest, to profess a belief in God is to subscribe to a theory that everything in existence can trace its origin back to one purposeful creative source, which continues to determine its composition and the way it operates.

Expanding on this, *The Modern Catholic Encyclopedia* refers to this source as 'God', which it describes as '…an object of worship and faith and an irreducible centre of meaning, power and value.' It is also stated to be 'the proper name for the "One" who creates and who thereby gives value to all that that has been created.' It is possible from this to view God as a single identifiable God who is transcendent (rising above, surmounting all) in capacity and immanent (ever-present, abiding) in application.[34]

---

34 *The Modern Catholic Encyclopedia* (Dublin: Gill & Macmillan, 1994), p347.

There is, of course, no way of proving any of this, but, by the same token, there is no conclusive means by which to disprove it. In the final analysis, it is for each person to decide whether or not the concept of God helps them to reach a better understanding of themselves, their relationships with others and the general circumstances of their lives. This will always be a free choice.

Looking back again to my childhood years, I remember being encouraged by my parents to think of God as a 'someone' to whom I could always turn rather than being some form of aloof, all-powerful and all-controlling entity. This worked for me then and it continues to do so now. I still have a myriad of questions of 'Why this?' or 'Why that?' in respect of creation and the general unfolding of life's events, but I am able to get on and enjoy life with what I regard as a rational explanation of why I am here and the comfort of believing that at least one of us in this relationship actually has all of the answers.

I recently came across a more expressive description of a personal relationship with God, which is attributed to St Alphonsus Liguori (1696–1787), the founder of the Redemptorist Order. In his words:

> 'Acquire the habit of speaking to God as if you are alone with Him; familiarly and with confidence and love, as to the most dearest of friends. Speak

to Him often of your business, your plans, your troubles, your fears – of everything that concerns you. Converse with Him confidently and frankly for God is not wont to speak to a soul that does not speak to Him.'[35]

In my experience, problems arise when people make 'absolute statements' about God or attempt to describe God by compiling lists of what they consider to be God's individual attributes, attitudes and approach to doing things and this is often further compounded when they attempt to impose their conclusions on other people. We need to accept that our intellect and vocabulary is incapable of bridging the divide between the finite us and the infinite that must be God in order for God to be God and not some larger-than-life human equivalent.

This was well expressed by St Thomas Aquinas (1225–1274), who stated that, 'We know *that* God is, not *what* God is. We know God only from God's effects.'[36] What we call the laws of nature are therefore expressions of God's activity in the universe and I consider that this is where we should direct our investigations in order to strengthen our belief in the existence of a purposeful and ever-abiding creative 'source'.

---

35 St Alphonsus Liguori parish website (Prospect Heights, Illinois, USA).
36 Referred to by Catherine Mowry LaCugna, *The Trinitarian Mystery of God* (Fortress, 1991), p158.

An ongoing process of discernment applies also to our understanding and appreciation of the Scriptures, but we sometimes seem to act as if we already know everything there is to know concerning God and God's purposes. As this has been described by Michael Morwood:

> '…we have fully worked out and put into neat theological categories all there is to know about God and all future questions and issues can be dealt within these categories. God's surprises are finished.'[37]

In presenting a case in support of a personal God, we need to begin by being honest and acknowledge that our faith story is exactly that – a matter of faith and trust. We are unable to produce irrefutable evidence for what we profess, but what we can do is to illustrate how and why we consider that this presumption offers a more inspirational reason than any of the others to explain our human presence and, in particular, our true potential as human beings.

As Christians, we have an added advantage of being able to refer to the life of Jesus in order to give shape to what we believe to be the underlying nature and purposes of our Creator God. This, too, must be

---

37 Michael Morwood, *Tomorrow's Catholic* (Spectrum Publications, 1997), p130.

accompanied by the admission that we are unable to prove what we claim to be the 'Father-Son' relationship between God and Jesus. All we can do is to highlight the way in which our outlook and daily experiences of life can be enhanced by attempting to follow and give practical expression to the message and example we have been given by Jesus.

Creation

To begin with what we are able to prove, there are now approaching eight billion of us human beings inhabiting planet Earth. We come in a variety of shapes, sizes and colours, but we all share the same physiological composition and, with the benefit of modern DNA testing, we have come to realise that we may be more closely related to one another than might previously have been imagined.

As a species, we possess two principal defining features – a faculty of 'reason', which enables us to draw conclusions from new or existing information, and a 'free will', which allows us to decide whether or not to implement whatever conclusions we reach. The former has enabled us to gain a position of ascendancy over other living species and to avail ourselves of the planet's resources in order to improve our quality of life in terms of education, health and comfort. The latter allows us the privilege of choice even though our decisions may not always be in our own best interests and might cause discomfort or even serious problems for others. We are eminently capable of making mistakes.

In terms of our origins, the Bible describes creation as a sequence of events that were instigated and managed by God over a seven-day period. This commenced with the provision of light out of darkness to comprise what we now call day and night and was followed by a separation of land from water and the emergence of food and other animals intended to support the arrival of our forebears, who are named as Adam and Eve. Their 'arrival' on the scene occurred on day six and the following day God is recorded as taking time off.

In contrast, we are reliably informed by science that the starting point for our universe was approximately fourteen billion years ago (allowing a possible margin of error of +/- two million years) when a subatomic particle self-activated to trigger an irreversible chain reaction that now accounts for everything that exists in our physical universe. This is popularly referred to as 'The Big Bang Theory' and is the product of numerous related scientific investigations over the years, which combined to arrive at this present conclusion in the early part of the 20th century.

I am happy to accept this given scientific explanation of our origin and all that has followed as a consequence subject to clarifying just two points of detail. The first is an explanation of where the subatomic particle is thought to have come from and the second is an explanation of what caused its seemingly random self-activation that thereby began 'time' as we now understand it.

The most straightforward and 'reasoned' answer for me is simply to insert the 'Theory of God' in chronological first position and credit God as the primary instigator of 'The Big Bang Theory' with its ensuing and ongoing process representing the chosen method of implementation. In this way I am able to explain the origin of the subatomic particle without in any way conflicting with or contradicting the inevitability of all subsequent physical events.

To highlight the sheer complexity of what we are dealing with here and to applaud the obvious expertise of the scientists who reached these conclusions, I consider that there is merit in providing a brief description of the immediate consequences of the Big Bang:

> '…in the first second, the start temperature fell to ten thousand million degrees (about 1,000 times hotter than the centre of our Sun) and over the next 90 seconds, dropped a further nine thousand million degrees. Protons and neutrons combined to produce helium and hydrogen in what could be described as a universal nuclear explosion which only ceased when there was insufficient heat to sustain further reactions.
>
> The universe continued to cool and expand

over the next million or so years and atoms began to form when the temperature had reduced to a few thousand degrees. The force of gravity then condensed matter to form the first stars and galaxies and nuclear reactions again started to occur in the interior of this first generation of stars.

The stars themselves eventually collapsed through tremendous explosions (supernova) to produce a second generation, spewing out heavier elements of carbon and iron which are essentials for life. Our own Sun is a second or third generation star which was thought to have been formed about four billion years ago from the debris of a supernova although more recent research indicates that the timing could be much closer to the earlier date of Big Bang itself. In any event, our sun is just one of several billion stars in our galaxy – and how many more galaxies might there still be to be discovered?'[38]

This factual account by science clearly rules out a literal interpretation of the Bible story, but in my view it does not negate its value as a figurative explanation to which people can more easily relate. I would suggest that a time frame measured in billions of years, temperatures of around ten thousand million degrees and an estimated distance

---

38 Ibid, p22.

of 18,921,600,000,000,000,000 kilometres between us and the biggest galaxy in our own cluster of thirty galaxies (Andromeda) are metrics that are well outside of most people's regular life experience.

I did more recently come across two alternative approaches to help reduce the difficulty in coming to terms with time and distance. The first of these was to treat creation as a twelve-month calendar year event in which:

> 'The Milky Way galaxy self-organised in late February and our solar system emerged from the elemental stardust of an exploded supernova in early September; planetary oceans formed in mid-September; Earth awakened into life in late September; sex was invented in late November; the dinosaurs lived for a few days in early December; and flowering plants burst on the scene with a dazzling array of colours in mid-December. The universe began reflecting consciously in and through human beings with choice and free will less than ten minutes before midnight on December 31st... We have known that we are in fact the Earth thinking about itself for less than a minute.
>
> On this scale of 12 months, Jesus would have been born on 31st December at approximately 11:59:45pm and the major scientific discoveries of the 20th and 21st centuries would have occurred

within the final second of the year. Similar to Genesis, this account adopts a descriptive currency to which people can more easily relate and within which we are now able to include scientific factors which were not available to the original author.'[39]

The second example to help come to terms with the issue of distance is to picture our own solar system of the Sun and its eight (prospectively nine) orbiting planets as being the size of a standard postage stamp. On this same scale, our galaxy as a whole would be equivalent to the land area of the United States of America or Australia.

Attempts such as these to try and reconcile religious and scientific explanations of our origins follow the approach of St Thomas Aquinas all those centuries ago known as 'The Five Ways'. This began with an assumption that the world mirrors God as its creator and then the rational implications of this are explored in terms of our experience of beauty, causality, signs of ordering and so forth, from which belief in God can be seen to offer a better empirical fit with the world around us than any of its alternatives. St Thomas did not claim proof of God's existence, simply that the appearance of design can offer serious persuasion concerning the divine creativity in the universe.

---

39   Ibid, p28.

Needless to say, our gift of 'free will' means that there will always be a variety of opinions and interpretations on a subject of this nature. There will be those who remain un-persuaded of any divine input, others who view the universe as an ongoing development in itself (Pantheism) or the work of an 'Intelligent Being', with functions left to their own devices (Deism). There are also Christians who regard the Bible story of creation recorded in Genesis as a literal account of the event.

The *Catechism of the Catholic Church* describes creation as being ordered (#299), of having its own goodness and proper perfection, of being in a state of journeying towards an ultimate perfection yet to be attained to which God has destined it (#302). The process by which God guides creation is termed 'Divine Providence' and is described as being '…concrete and immediate and covering the least things to the great events of the world and its history; an affirmation of God's absolute sovereignty over the course of all events' (#303).

At face value this could suggest that divine providence is an inbuilt element of God's design, which determines how each event will, and indeed how they *must*, unfold, but the text goes on to state that out of love for humankind, we are the exception. That we have been granted the dignity to act on our own, of being causes and principles for each other as well as co-workers with God to complete the work of creation and perfect its harmony (#306/307).

This surely represents a major boost to our self-esteem as a species and should act as an encouragement to work more closely with each other for our collective benefit.

Evolution

According to the Bible, God created Adam and Eve on the sixth day of creation and placed them as fully grown adults in a pre-prepared environment. As described in the *Catechism*, they were created in God's own image (#355), the only creatures willed for their own sake and able to share by knowledge and love in God's own life (#356).

The *Catechism* goes on to state that Adam and Eve were created good and established in friendship with their Creator, in harmony with themselves and with creation around them, as well as being in an original state of holiness and justice in order to share in divine life (#374/375). They were unimpaired and ordered in their own being because they were free of the triple concupiscence that subjects them to the pleasure of the senses, covetousness for earthly goods and self-assertion contrary to the dictates of reason (#377).

Leaving aside for the moment how we claim to know all of these things about our original forebears, we are forced to conclude from this description that humankind was intended to be a highly specified and privileged species, and was purposely 'installed' as such by God to take pole position in His plan for creation. In contrast, the 'Theory of Evolution' considers the possibility of a different route by which humankind has achieved its ascendancy and is concerned with explaining why individual species are as they are by proposing a general unified account of how different species are related.

The term 'evolution' is usually associated with the naturalist Charles Darwin (1809–82) whose findings were that species do not always remain the same over time. They are mutable and undergo repeated changes and adaptations to their environment. Whilst this is not a proven demonstrated certainty, there is so much that the theory does explain that biologists are virtually unanimous in accepting it.

The inevitable question is whether this conflicts with the Christian doctrine of creation and, specifically, the explanation for our human presence. The answer to this will depend upon the terms of reference we adopt, as if we insist on a literal reading of the Bible, we will have to conclude that the scientific community is wrong or that the available evidence can be explained in a different way. Alternatively, if we accept that the Bible is not intended to be a scientific treatise but rather a means of attempting to express a relationship between God and humankind, then a meeting point is a possibility.

As this is described in *The Modern Catholic Encyclopedia*, the doctrine of creation is not a story about the beginning of the world as an event that has already happened, but a statement of belief that each thing in existence and each event that occurs is because God knows and wills its existence and occurrence. In other words, it is a relation of dependence such that neither the universe nor any of its component parts to include evolution is entirely self-explanatory. The only complete explanation of why things are as they happen to be is because God created them so.[40]

On this basis, it is possible to assert with confidence that the whole of creation – which is generally agreed to have come into being from nothing – must, by necessity, be entirely permeated with God's presence as this is the only source from which everything (beginning with the subatomic particle) could have derived its existence. Within this broad understanding, it then becomes possible to view the entire universe as a single process of evolutionary development moving on from the Big Bang through elemental particles to molecules to organisms to persons. In the words of the American theologian Sally McFague:

---

40 *The Modern Catholic Encyclopedia* (Dublin: Gill & Macmillan, 1994), p301.

> 'All of us living and non-living are one phenomenon, a phenomenon stretching over billions of years and containing untold numbers of strange, diverse and marvellous forms of matter – including our own. The universe is a body, to use a poor analogy from our own experience, but it is not a human body, rather it is matter bodied forth, seemingly infinitely, diversely, endlessly, yet internally as one.'[41]

This is a description that could be said to echo St Paul's account of God as Father of all, over all, through all and within all, who descended to the lowest regions of the earth so that rising He might fill all things (Ephesians 4:9–10). It was this Pauline passage that influenced the 20th-century Jesuit theologian and scientist, Teilhard de Chardin (1881–1955), in his search to resolve what, for him, were the two apparently conflicting attractions involving the impersonal world of matter known by science and the revealed word of God known by faith.

Thus, through St Paul, we have revelation telling of God descending into the world of matter, and science telling how matter rose into spirit through the theory of evolution. How the impersonal world of matter became reflectively conscious as ourselves, rather than

---

[41] Referred to by Michael Morwood, *Tomorrow's Catholic* (Spectrum Publications, 1997), p39.

us considering ourselves to be an entirely independent and self-contained species that simply emerged as such at a specific point in time.

Within this 'interconnected' model of creation, it is possible to see everything as being infused with, sustained by and driven by the energy that is of God and serves to reinforce the long-standing Christian belief that humankind, with our unique and distinctive features of reason and free will, must be more intimately related to God than simply being a physical end product of a creative process. As this is described by Michael Morwood:

> '…we can identify ourselves in terms of its reality, devise significance and give meaning to our lives, marvel at who and what we are, give praise on behalf of all creation and allow this faith to shape our lives and the destiny of life on this planet.'[42]

Our relatedness to a Creator God was a key element in the theology of another 20th-century theologian, Karl Rahner (1904–84), who regarded this as being so deeply built into us, so critical in making us what we are that nothing we do would be possible without it. In Rahner's view, being related to God, whether we realise it or not, is so much part of our structure that it is not

---

42   Ibid, p36.

possible to describe what it is to love or to will or even to think about it in a human fashion without bringing God into the description.

Clearly, Rahner's views may not be shared by every scientist specialising in quantum physics, but from a Christian perspective it does suggest how we might better appreciate the notion of God's continuing presence. Under this arrangement, God is not to be understood as an external and remote overseer or manipulator of events who rewards and punishes, but as having an incarnational presence that operates in, with and through what God has to work with – namely, each of us. We are frequently reminded that we have been created in the image and likeness of God, but how much thought do we give, or are we encouraged to give, to what this might actually entail?

In the early Church, 'image' was seen to be a permanent feature of humankind, whilst 'likeness' became viewed as our image in action and therefore liable to change – to progress or regress or even disappear as a result of a person's actions. As described by Gerald O'Collins, '…whatever human beings are in God's image they are, and cannot not be, because if they were to cease to be God's image they could no longer be human.'[43]

Being created in the image of God is therefore

---

[43] Gerald O'Collins, *Jesus Our Redeemer: A Christian Approach to Salvation* (Oxford University Press, 2007), p25.

at the heart of being human and as such I consider that it calls for a more expansive explanation than we currently receive from our pastoral leadership. We need to be helped to recapture the essence of the Church's earlier theology of our image being an invitation for each of us to participate in God's own being rather than simply regarding ourselves as subscribers to a given set of ecclesial directives. As a religious mystery, this invites a lifetime of reflection and we can never expect to fully argue everything out in complete and final detail, but this is no excuse in the meantime for inadequate exegesis.

Moreover, a better appreciation that we are all formed in God's image reinforces the understanding that we are part of the same family. That we should remain ever conscious of the needs of others and be willing to act accordingly when support is needed. As Scripture reminds us: 'To act virtuously and with justice is more pleasing to Yahweh than sacrifice' (Proverbs 21:3).

Religion and Science

Over recent centuries, science has progressively captured the centre ground of public opinion in claiming to provide definitive answers to questions concerning our world by methodical process rather than relying on mere hypotheses, which are sometimes suggested as being all that is on offer from the Church.

This has been further encouraged by what has been seen as a tendency by our pastoral leadership to view new scientific findings with suspicion or as a potential threat to Christian orthodoxy and, on occasions, has caused them to express views on matters that are outside their remit and competence.

The 16th-century dispute between the Church and Galileo is a well-known example. In this case, the scientific proposition that the earth travels round the sun rather than being the fixed centrepiece of creation was opposed on the grounds that it was in direct conflict with a literal translation of a specific phrase within the Bible. It took several centuries before the Church formally apologised for its treatment of Galileo.

Effectively, religion and science seek different answers about our world. Science will seek to explain how the world came about and answer in terms of the Big Bang whereas religion will be more interested in why the universe is here at all and answer this in terms of a Creator God and God's own purposes. Science is concerned with the physical world of material things and events and looks for explanations concerning matter and energy that can be counted, weighed and measured to see how it works – namely, its mechanism. Religion seeks answers to such things as meanings, purposes and values.[44]

---

44   Ernest Lucas, *Can We Believe Genesis Today?* (Inter-Varsity Press, 2001) p14 and 31.

Writing in the 1940s, Albert Einstein held that:

> 'Science can only ascertain what is but not what should be, and outside of its domain value judgements of all kinds remain necessary. Religion on the other hand deals only with evaluations of human thought and actions; it cannot justifiably speak of facts and relationships between facts. According to this interpretation, the well-known conflicts between religion and science in the past can be ascribed to a misapprehension of the situation which has been described.'[45]

The Vatican II document, *Gaudium et Spes*, makes it clear that if methodical investigation in any branch of knowledge is carried out in a genuinely scientific manner and in accord with moral laws, it need never be in conflict with our faith in God. This is because the things of the world and the things of faith derive from the same God, as do the 'humble and persevering investigators' (GS #36). The document goes on to criticise short-sighted attitudes concerning the rightful autonomy of science, which from time to time have occasioned conflict and controversy and misled many into opposing faith and science.

---

45 From the website 'Albert Einstein, Religion and Science', a symposium published following the conference on 'Science, Philosophy and Religion in Their Relation to the Democratic Way of Life', 1941.

I consider that religion and science have a legitimate place alongside each other in the human quest for truth and meaning. Science is one aspect of the human faculty of reason and theology is another. The former seeks to explain *how* things work, the latter attempts to offer explanations concerning *why*. Both disciplines should operate in concert representing different sides of the same coin – perhaps sometimes in tension, but not always assumed to be in perpetual opposition.

It is perhaps interesting to record that one of the foremost proponents of Big Bang was the Belgian scientist Georges Lemaitre (1894–1966), who was also a Catholic priest. Moreover, the highly regarded 20th-century Harvard physicist and scientific historian, Stanley Jaki (1924–2009), also happened to be a priest and his considered view was that the scientific quest only found fertile ground when faith in a personal rational Creator had truly permeated an entire culture. It was this faith that provided, in sufficient measure, the indispensable ingredients of confidence in the rationality of the universe, trust in progress and an appreciation of the quantitative method of research.

In summary, I believe that the whole of creation is the product of a single defining purpose – a purpose I refer to as 'God'. I regard this as a rational explanation for everything that I can see, hear and experience and the more that we discover and understand about the workings of our physical environment, the more convinced I become. In my view, the universe is too big, too complex, too interconnected and too continuously active to simply be thought of as a random occurrence.

I believe also that this Creator God wished to be known by us and chose to do this by means of our gifted inbuilt human faculties of reason and free will; faculties that are fully exemplified in the person of Jesus. The message we can confidently draw from this is that we do not have to search for God because he is already present within us as an intrinsic element of what it is to be human and we do not always need to try and impress God by our own efforts because He loves us for precisely who and what he made us to be. We should instead be grateful for what we have been given and concentrate on how we should treat each other as members of a single extended family by the way in which we exercise our own free will.

This is the faith story that we, as the Church, should be proclaiming in our 21st-century world, but in practice we seem to place greater emphasis on promoting the 'omnipotent otherness' of God rather than His 'personal relatedness' to each of us. God is fully aware of His transcendence without having to be reminded of it by us, whereas many people continue to be the poorer because they are unaware of the closeness of God's presence in their daily lives.

THE INCARNATION OF JESUS

Christianity is about the life, death and resurrection of Jesus. We proclaim our belief each Sunday in the words of our ancient Nicene-Constantinopolitan Creed:

> '...Only Son of God... eternally begotten... of one being with the Father... for our salvation came down from Heaven... became incarnate from the Virgin Mary... suffered death and was buried... rose again... ascended to Heaven... is seated at the right hand of the Father... will come again in glory to judge the living and the dead.'

These are the faith statements we recite week in and week out, but I wonder how much attention we give, or are encouraged to give, to the origins and significance of these individual expressions? What do they tell us about the reason for the incarnation, about Jesus as a person and the implications for us? To consider these questions individually:

The Purpose of the Incarnation

This is stated in the *Penny Catechism* as being 'to redeem us from sin and hell and to teach us the way to Heaven' (#43). This required Jesus to suffer death on the cross in order to 'atone for our sins and to purchase eternal life on our behalf' (#55). A connection is made between the sin of Adam and the crucifixion of Jesus, which is seen as the necessary price to restore us to God's favour and to repair the breach in what had previously been a totally harmonious relationship between God and humanity.

So what sort of picture does this present? We start with the Bible account of God's gift of creation in which humankind is described as being 'very good' (Gen 1:2), but in relatively short order our first parents managed to blight our collective copybook by their reported act of disobedience. This offended God to the extent that his forgiveness was deemed to call for suitable prior amends, but because we had become a 'flawed species' we could not achieve this by our own efforts. As a result, we were given a second gift from God in the person of His Son Jesus, who was dispatched to Earth to become one of us and to suffer and die on the cross in order to wipe the slate clean from all previous sins and as payment on account for all likely future sins.

God raised Jesus from the dead so that as 'fellow human beings' we might again become eligible for God's original offer of eternal life. The extent of God's love was evidenced by the suffering that His Son was called upon to endure on our behalf and we are left in little doubt as to the challenges we will be called upon to face as part of life's ongoing battle between the forces of good and evil.

This formed the essential framework for my Catholic upbringing. We were urged to count ourselves fortunate to have been given a second chance in the person of Jesus, but this was understood as wholly conditional upon us following His Church's prescribed liturgical practices and moral precepts. Failure to maintain a 'clean record' would serve as a reminder of our personal responsibility for Jesus's suffering, as well as highlighting our need to rely on God's mercy in order to minimise the degree of punishment that might otherwise be in prospect. It is small wonder that we Catholics were often considered to be perpetually guilt-ridden.

Decades later, the *Catechism of the Catholic Church* continues to expound on the same theme of sin and retribution. That Jesus's death 'was not the result of chance or an unfortunate coincidence of circumstances but is part of the mystery of God's plan' (#599). It then proceeds to describe the death of Jesus as the 'Pascal Sacrifice that accomplishes the definitive redemption of man' and 'the Sacrifice of the New Covenant which restores man to communion with God by reconciling him to God through the blood of the covenant which was poured out for many for the forgiveness of sins' (#613). The sacrifice of Jesus is explained as 'a gift from God Himself who hands His Son to sinners in order to reconcile us with Himself and His Son offers his life in freedom and love to the Father in reparation for our disobedience' (#614).

So what sort of picture does this create for later generations of Catholics? In my view, much the same as before, namely that Jesus was a necessary time-specific contingency to compensate for our continuing bad behaviour. In reality, I would not expect God's plan would ever have to admit to a need for any such mid-course corrections. He will have been fully aware from the outset how human affairs would evolve.

A second cause for concern is the frequent reference to God being 'offended' – as based on the usual understanding of the word, this would represent an affront to a person's pride or dignity. How can this apply when speaking about God? And yet the prayer we were taught to memorise and use at confession called for us to '…detest our sins most of all because they offended God's infinite goodness'. I find it difficult also to believe that an 'offended' God would purposely wish to prolong an extensive period of displeasure, but our *Penny Catechism* stated that '...even the just were excluded from Heaven until this was opened for them by Jesus' (#65).

Thirdly, and for me the most uncomfortable aspect of what had been my early catechetical teaching, was how Jesus's death was presented as its own self-description. In other words it was a sacrificial act that met the predetermined criteria deemed necessary to make amends for our sins. By implication therefore, it was an act that must have been specified by God as His minimum reserve price for our redemption, as how else would the criteria have been identified or for what other purpose was the price to be paid? What an astonishing view of God this presents!

From the earliest times in human history there is evidence of sacrifices being offered to appease a deity or in order to gain a favour. The *Old Testament* abounds with examples of sin-offerings and communion offerings but in my view there is a vast difference between a death that is presumed to represent an end in itself and a death that followed as a result of what Jesus said and did. As this is described by Gerald O'Collins: 'The sacrifice of Jesus was not due to his positive and direct will (or that of his Father), but to the abuse of human freedom on the part of the religious and political leaders at the time whose vested interests were threatened by his uncompromising message.'[46]

---

46 Gerald O'Collins, *Jesus our Redeemer: A Christian Approach to Salvation* (Oxford University Press, 2007), p171.

In my view, greater emphasis needs to be given to the life, death and resurrection of Jesus as wholly interrelated components of a single God-given experience for human kind. The underlying purpose for the incarnation can then be seen as being to proclaim the nearness of God to people's day-by-day existence and to show us how we can and should live our lives. I consider that this is well expressed by the *Modern Catholic Encyclopedia*:

> 'When Jesus ate with outcasts and sinners, when he ministered amongst the peasants of Galilea, when he challenged the religious and social patterns of exclusivity, domination and self-righteousness and replaced them with ones based on compassion and when he involved men and women in a radically inclusive community of disciples, God's salvation was already present and being made manifest'.[47]

It is also evident from the stories of healings that came about through the actions of Jesus that salvation was not confined to purely religious considerations but involved liberation from all that oppresses and enslaves people. In the words of Michael Morwood:

> 'Jesus understood his ministry in terms of setting people free… His life and death were not

---

[47] *The Modern Catholic Encyclopedia* (Dublin: Gill & Macmillan, 1994), p794.

connected with changing God's mind or winning back God's friendship. Rather, his living and dying were about changing people's minds and hearts… that in Jesus's preaching, salvation is connected with setting people free from fear, ignorance and darkness and with changing how they formed an image or thought about God and themselves.'[48]

Against this background, I consider that the way in which Church teaching on the incarnation continues to be presented can give rise to several confusing messages:

1. We are taught that God is infinite love and compassion, but He is also portrayed as requiring due recompense for our sinfulness. Could this imply that God loved humanity less before the incarnation?
2. The death and resurrection of Jesus can be seen as a high point in God's unfolding plan, but the emphasis often placed on the sacrificial nature of our deliverance from evil can result in salvation appearing to be a process or a formula, rather than a person (or more correctly, three divine persons) acting with boundless love.
3. The emphasis on the passion and death of Jesus adds further weight to the notion that

---

[48] Michael Morwood, *Tomorrow's Catholic* (Spectrum Publications, 1997), p79.

the sole purpose of the incarnation was to satisfy a remote and offended God. What could be further from the true picture of our God whose forgiveness was never in doubt and who chose to express this in a manner that is wholly compatible with our human gift of freedom.

4. Whilst Jesus is described as both divine and human, the latter can come across as the 'junior partner' in this arrangement and lessen the inspirational impact of what he said and did in acting with a human will and loving with a human heart (GS #22). The emphasis on Jesus's divinity is understandable given that questions concerning this belief have been the most prevalent over the centuries, but I consider that we need to recover an improved balance that avoids Jesus only appearing to be human – 'a mythical divine' who is simply acting out a human charade.'[49]

5. A constant emphasis on the sinfulness of humankind and the codified status of sin can result in life appearing to be a continuous route march across a minefield of mortal and venial sins that are about to explode. We cannot ignore evil in our world but it can be equally damaging

---

49 Robert A. Burns; *Roman Catholicism after Vatican II* (Georgetown University Press, 2001), p21.

to become preoccupied with the topic. I take comfort from the suggestion by the Anglican Bishop of Durham, N. T. Wright, that '...evil may be a four letter word, but so too, thank God, is love'.[50]

The paradox for me is that the official explanation of the incarnation seems to manifest the sort of negative, restrictive and self-righteous mindset that Jesus sought to dispel by virtue of becoming incarnate.

The Person of Jesus

The Gospel of St Mark recounts the story of an angel appearing to Mary to ask her to bear a son who would come into being purely by the power of God and who was to be given the name, Jesus. Mary is recorded to have replied, 'Let what you have said be done to me' (Mt 1:26–38), and so the story of Jesus of Nazareth can be said to have begun.

Jesus was born in Bethlehem and grew up in Nazareth with Mary, his mother, and Joseph, his acting father. In adult life he became a teacher in the style of the ancient Jewish heralds or prophets, being continuously on the move in order to repeat his message (*kerygma*) and to deliver an instruction (*didakhe*) to as many people as

---

50   N.T. Wright, *Evil and the Justice of God* (SPCK, 2006), p56.

possible. His essential message was that the kingdom of God was close at hand and that people should repent and believe in the Scriptures (Mark 11:14–15).

I take the reference to the closeness of the kingdom of God as being to emphasise that God's intention is to be forever close to each of us through all of the ups and downs of our daily lives, rather than being thought of as a remote overseer or judge. The word 'repent' in its biblical context would have been understood to mean making an effort to effect a change in outlook in one's mind, heart and purpose, and clearly the Scriptures were understood to be a guide to help achieve this.

As time progressed, the message of Jesus and his popularity among the people was seen by many of the religious leaders to represent a challenge as well as a potential threat to their authority as the recognised official interpreters of the Law of Moses. This prompted them to conspire with the Civil Authorities to find cause against Jesus, which eventually resulted in him being charged, found guilty, sentenced and put to death by means of crucifixion.

For many of Jesus's followers, this was a disappointing end to what had appeared to be the long-awaited promise of God to send a Messiah to be the saviour and liberator of the Jewish people. But it was a story that did not end with a crucifixion, death and internment, as stories soon began to circulate that Jesus had been raised from the dead and that this could be supported by a number of verified sightings. A belief in the risen Jesus continued to grow and transform the lives of those who had remained loyal to his memory and others who had since become attracted to his reported legacy.

Human nature being what it is, the way in which Jesus was remembered could, on occasions, be coloured by what might be termed 'post-resurrection enthusiasm' and which sometimes admitted to exaggerations and even misinterpretations. The previously mentioned Ecumenical Councils at Nicaea, Constantinople, Ephesus and Chalcedon were therefore necessary means in seeking to establish the orthodox doctrine concerning the nature and purposes of Jesus and his life with us.

As for Jesus himself, he was born and brought up in the Jewish faith and his outlook will undoubtedly have reflected the Judaism of the time in the context of its historical background and approach to religious observance. His message was not in conflict with Jewish Law but introduced a new way for it to be understood and applied. This might be described as adding a subjective dimension to what had become an increasingly objective and legalistic interpretation of God's Covenant.

Jesus called people to consider more than just the letter of the Law by introducing a pastoral dimension to purely juridical interpretations of individual texts. He also declared it to be an offer that was open to all peoples, not simply one select group.

The uniqueness of Jesus's ministry was his total dedication to the service of others, which he undertook in complete obedience to his sending by his Father. So closely did his life correspond to what he had been sent to say and do that he himself could be said to be that message – the living Word of God.[51]

Jesus did not simply teach about worship, he was in his very being the perfect example of what worship is. In the words of Michael Richards, 'Here was a man involved in all aspects of contemporary life, subjected to the same temptations as we are but acting always and in every way as the Law and the Temple were meant to bring people to act.'[52]

To cite the Epistle to the Hebrews, Jesus was described as the apostle and high priest of our religion (3:1); a priest by virtue of his example rather than a law of descent and a priest forever according to the higher order of Melchizedek (7:16–18). He led a blameless and uncontaminated life, which attained what earlier sacrifices failed to achieve, and he could be said to mark the fulfilment of the old law by signalling a new beginning for us as the source of eternal salvation (5:9–10).

The *Catechism of the Catholic Church* informs us that the name 'Jesus' means 'God saves' in Hebrew and

---

[51] Michael Richards, *A People of Priests: The Ministry of the Catholic Church* (Darton, Longman & Todd, 1995), p.73.
[52] Ibid, p28.

that this expresses his identity and mission (#430). The word 'Christ' from the Greek translation of the Hebrew word 'Messiah' means 'anointed one' and becomes the name proper to Jesus because he perfectly accomplished the divine mission that Christ signifies (#436).

In the Gospel accounts of Jesus's baptism and transfiguration, he is referred to by God as His 'Blessed Son', which affirms his eternal pre-existence (#444). The Greek equivalent of the name originally used by God to reveal Himself to Moses is *Kyrios* or 'Lord' and serves to indicate the divinity of Israel's God. The same title of Lord is stated in the Gospels to relate to both the Father and Jesus, who is thereby to be recognised as God himself (#446).

We have now identified the complete doctrinal title: 'Lord Jesus Christ, Son of God'. However, I consider that the initial impression that could be conveyed by these several definitions and descriptions is that God is simply acting out an event in history under the guise of a human appearance. What could be termed a 'top-down' approach in which the humanity of Jesus is merely circumstantial.

The *Catechism* then proceeds to describe Jesus enjoying, in his human knowledge, '*the fullness*' (my emphasis) of the eternal plan he had come to reveal (#474), which seems to add further support to this circumstantial notion in the absence of any explanation of how this knowledge is thought to have come about.

One school of thought is that because of the 'hypostatic union' of the divine and human (see Council of Chalcedon, p11), Jesus was not in any way limited in his knowledge, but if this is the case it would surely represent yet another difference between him and us.

An alternative view is that Jesus had an intuitive knowledge of who he was but had to acquire the ability to express this to himself and then to others over time.[53] This seems more compatible with the opinion expressed by St Paul that 'although Jesus's state was divine, he did not cling to his equality with God but emptied himself (the Greek word being *kenosis*) to assume the condition of a slave and became as men are' (Philippians 2:6–7). Vatican II in its turn speaks of Jesus working with human hands, thinking with a human mind, acting with a human will and loving with a human heart, and thereby fully revealing humanity to itself (GS #25).

A second observation on the *Catechism* account is that it provides little to help us know Jesus in the sense of our affinity with him as a fellow human being. We are simply provided with a name and a set of titles, together with a description of what these are intended to signify. Generally speaking, when we talk of 'knowing' someone it means being aware of what it is that makes them tick as a person and how this

---

53   Robert Burns, 'Roman Catholicism after Vatican II, p22.

is likely to influence the way in which they act or are likely to react to particular situations.

Contrast the description of Jesus provided by Karen Kilby, that '...if being orientated towards God is what makes us human then the one who is so orientated that he is utterly given over to God and utterly taken over by God, is actually the one who is at the same time the most fully human. Jesus can be seen as the supreme example of this and in his openness to God, God's self-communication is met with a free and perfect response.'[54] I would imagine that this is what the bishops at Vatican II actually had in mind when they spoke of Jesus revealing humanity to itself.

Jesus needs to be understood also as the presence of God's saving activity in the world in such a way that he is seen to be part of the world, not an external deity breaking into human affairs at a particular point in time. The essential premise as described by Karen Kilby is that Jesus is not the trigger for God to become gracious but the peak of God being gracious, a high point in the history of salvation rather than a turning point.[55]

The *Old Testament* abounds with examples of God's actions through history with the concept of 'Wisdom' (in Greek, *Sophia* – and female!) being associated with all creative works as well as serving to help overcome the acute sense of the divide between the transcendent

---

54 Karen Kilby, *Karl Rahner* (Fount Publishing, 1997), p19.
55 Ibid, p27.

otherness of God and the divine presence or immanence perceived in creation. By the time of the *New Testament*, the title of wisdom was being ascribed to Jesus to reflect that his life, death and resurrection had generated a 'new creation' of graced life for everyone (Romans 1:6).

As a result, Jesus became recognised as one and the same agent for both the 'original creation' recorded in Genesis as well as this 'new creation', which followed as a result of his resurrection. In the words of St Paul: 'He (God) has let us know the mystery of His purpose, the hidden plan He so kindly made in Christ from the beginning… and it is in him that we were claimed as God's own, chosen from the beginning' (Eph 1: 9–11).

Jesus is therefore an intrinsic element of God's being (eternally begotten) and when spoken of synonymously with Wisdom he can be identified as the principal implementer of creation. This, of course, is what we profess in our weekly *Credo,* that '…through him all things were made', but I wonder how many Catholics pick up on these words and appreciate the connectedness between Creation and the Incarnation, and its significance for us?

Specifically, that the Word/Wisdom/Son of God/Jesus can be understood as the prototype for humanity, in that we are all created in this same image and likeness. That the incarnation of Jesus was always part of the plan irrespective of the actions of Adam and that he defines our relationship to God, to each other and the rest of creation. Humanity understands itself in God's own light and finds its ultimate fulfilment in following a lifelong pilgrimage to reach the fullness of this goal.

A remaining 'credibility target' to try and resolve for our 21st-century world is how to explain the means by which an identifiable embryo was formed in a female womb with the same physiological composition as all other human embryos but without any male involvement. We know from today's medical science that to be human, Jesus will have been born with his own unique DNA profile of forty-six individual chromosomes of which half will have been inherited from his mother. But what about the other half?

We need to admit that there is no simple answer here or any means by which to supply irrefutable genetic evidence for proper scientific investigation. The Jesus of history is a matter of record but we are unable to point to a seamless connection with the Jesus of faith. All we have to offer is that our belief in a cosmic order suggests an ultimate sufficient reason: a cosmic Orderer who thereby defines and implements all of the rules.[56]

The Implications of the Incarnation for Us

If one is willing for the moment to accept the claim that Jesus is both divine and human, it becomes

---

56 Gerald O'Collins, *Jesus our Redeemer: A Christian Approach to Salvation* (Oxford University Press, 2007), p36.

important to give further thought to how we describe and understand his second nature, since by necessity this has a direct bearing on us as fellow human beings. So, for example, if we regard human nature as being wholly definable, something that can be set within boundaries and precisely specified, nothing more than a product of forty-six individual chromosomes, it is not clear how an infinite and omniscient God could become so circumscribed and delimited, and still in any sense be God.[57]

By contrast, if we revisit the earlier mentioned theology of Karl Rahner, then human nature is not seen as being closed in on itself but is instinctively able to consider meaning, values and purpose, and to comprise a kind of infinite openness, which is always striving beyond the finite to that which is beyond the world; to what Rahner refers to as a holy mystery – to God. In his view, when we have said everything about ourselves that can be described and defined, we have still said nothing until we have included or implied that we are beings that are referred to the incomprehensible God.

This again points us towards understanding Jesus as the prototype for what it is to be human rather than being a 'human facsimile' in order for God to make Himself visible. The divinity of Jesus belongs to him as something unique and absolute, but on the other hand

---

[57] Karen Kilby, *Karl Rahner* (Fount Publishing, 1997), p26.

it can be situated within the broader phenomenon of the common humanity of us all. In other words, Jesus is the extreme case of what it is to be human, like us only more so, what we are if we take it all the way to its limit. Again, what a boost this should be for our individual self-esteem and what better way to remind us of the responsibility we thereby owe to one another.

A greater emphasis on the human aspect of Jesus could be termed a 'bottom-up' approach. Under this scenario, we are able to see ourselves as being related to God through the person of Jesus with whom we share the same image and likeness and therefore the opportunity to participate in His divine life through our gifts of knowledge, freedom and love. As this is described by W. Dyche, 'Human beings came to be so that God can share his life in this way. We were not simply created and left to get on with life with God's self-revelation (grace) hovering above us as an added embellishment, but rather this revelation is embedded within the deepest identity of humankind.'[58]

A greater focus on the human dimension of Jesus also enables us to better appreciate our own inbuilt potential based on his inspiration and encouragement as a fellow human being. We can relate to Jesus as someone who understands the trials and tribulations of the human condition, having experienced them in

---

[58] W. Dych, 'Transcendental Theology' in *Karl Rahner* (Liturgical Press, 1992), p72.

the same way as us. I believe this is well expressed by Robert Burns that in reaching out to Jesus one is really reaching out to touch a brother, but is, at the same time, being touched and embraced by God himself.[59]

And to strengthen our understanding of this relatedness, we were invited by Jesus to address God as *Abba* ('Father') and in so doing we are introduced to the 'Theology of Divinisation' – the view that Jesus, who was divine, became truly human so that we, as humans, could visualise ourselves as being divine by virtue of grace and adoption.

This is a concept that does actually receive a mention in the *Catechism of the Catholic Church* but as just one of several reasons to explain the incarnation. Predictably, our list begins by describing Jesus's task to reconcile us to God by being the expiation for our sins (#457); to show us God's love (#458); and to be our model of holiness (#459). Then finally, and for me the most compelling reason, which warrants being quoted in full, is that:

> 'The Word became flesh to make us partakers of the divine nature. For this is why the Word became man and the Son of God became the Son of man; so that man, by entering into communion with the Word and thus receiving divine sonship, might

---

[59] Robert A. Burns, *Roman Catholicism after Vatican II* (Georgetown University Press, 2001), p23.

become a son of God. For the Son of God became man so that we might become God. The only begotten Son of God, wanting to make us sharers in His divinity, assumed our nature, so that he made man, might make men Gods' (#460).

This has to comprise a life-changing notion to attempt to take on board and almost begs the question of whether we will ever be able to fully achieve such an understanding? This is particularly the case for those of us who were brought up on a regular diet of personal sin and failure, which continuously disfigured the original image and likeness of God in our souls.

What a difference it could make if 'divinisation' is presented as *the* defining purpose for the incarnation to thereby establish a positive overall framework within which to rank the other explanations. That rather than the starting point always being our inherent sinfulness, which needs to be pardoned, our focus could be directed more towards God's unbounded love for each of us in whom he sees the image of His Son, Jesus.

In his brief period of public ministry, Jesus asked people to examine the way in which they lived their lives and he called on them to pursue a change of heart and mind. I consider that our attention over recent centuries has become focused more on the latter in seeking to categorise, rationalise and issue judgement calls on patterns of behaviour. Now could be an ideal time to put 'heart' back into the equation and restore a more balanced individual and collective outlook. In the words of St Paul:

> 'If I have all the eloquence of men or of angels, but speak without love, I am simply a gong booming or a cymbal clashing. If I have the gift of prophecy, understanding all the mysteries there are and knowing everything, and if I have faith in all its fullness, to move mountains but without love then I am nothing at all. If I give away all that I possess, piece by piece and if I even let them take my body to burn it but am without love, it will do me no good whatever' (Cor 12:13, 13:1–13).

SIN

It will be evident from the two previous chapters that the Catholic psyche is seriously influenced by our attitude towards sin. This seems to be based on a dualistic notion (remember *Gnosticism*!) of two distinct worlds – one 'divine', the other 'profane' – which insists that the true form of our humanity is set in a previous lost paradise or in a future age after this world has ended. It holds that to be human is to go radically astray, to be wrong-footed from the start, to be flawed as a result of a first sin at the beginning of time. It refuses to accept ignorance, mortality and mistakes as a normal condition of humanity.[60]

We also have a tendency to regard sin as the driving force of God's involvement in history. It was sin that led to the 'fall' and our expulsion from the Garden of

---

60 Daniel O' Leary. *Lost Soul? The Catholic Church Today* (The Columbia Press, 1999), p29.

Eden. It was sin that was seen as the underlying cause of the misfortunes of the Israelites and led eventually to the giving of the law on Sinai. The crucifixion and death of Jesus is viewed as the unavoidable response to the problem caused by sin.

I am in no way doubting the existence of sin, simply the way in which we seem to be encouraged to give it expression. By way of example, my parish subscribed some years ago to a series of pamphlets with the stated aim of enabling us to rediscover and study the fundamental content of our faith.[61] The pattern was set by the initial pamphlet in which the opening statement read: 'From before the beginning of time, God had a plan to save us from our sins'.

Once again, I question how we claim to know about such things as God's initial plan and in this instance, there is the suggestion that it was necessary for God to make an allowance for sin before it ever occurred; as if sin already existed in some form of higher order of things and would inevitably become manifest in the behaviour of humankind. So much for the notion of God as the Supreme Creator.

A subsequent pamphlet was concerned with 'The four things always to be remembered'. This is a title that I certainly can remember from my *Penny Catechism*, namely Death, Judgement, Heaven and Hell (#332).

---

[61] 'Adult Formation and Catechesis in the Year of Faith' (The Association for Catechumenal Ministry, 2012).

This served to caution that whilst Heaven is our intended destiny, not all of us would make it and for some people their sins would result in them spending eternity in a condition of unimaginable pain and suffering. Strong stuff at the time for impressionable seven- and eight-year-olds!

My concern today is that the use of unqualified or poorly explained statements of this nature can create a negative and misleading image of God, of ourselves and of other people. It perpetuates a view of God as being a remote and purely judgemental entity and we might easily come to see ourselves as undeserving or even as failures because of our propensity to sin. Catholics in my generation were often inclined (or was it encouraged?) to regard the world outside the Church with suspicion, as if everything there must, in some way, be contaminated by sin.

Defining Sin

The *Modern Catholic Encyclopedia* describes 'sin' as a word used to express a moral evil when seen in the context of religion as distinct from ethics or civil law. The Christian ideal is to do everything 'as done to the Lord', so shortcomings are judged to be against a divinely given law and defined as the free and deliberate disobedience of a creature to the known will of God. Sin is therefore primarily a religious or theological reality, a symbol that expresses our alienation from God.[62]

As a symbol, sin has been the subject of continuous historical and cultural development from biblical time onwards, and it could be fair to say that the word itself has become somewhat trivialised in today's more secular-orientated world. Even within religious circles, the word can tend to be associated mainly with acts or events connected with sexual behaviour.

In the Catholic tradition, sin is very much related to confession with a particular focus on guilt. As all sin is judged as disobedience to God (and to one's lawful superiors), a strong emphasis on obedience is an established feature of Catholic life, which calls for a regular examination of conscience to identify possible infidelity to the laws of God and the Church. For some people this can be a worrying exercise of daily soul-searching for possible transgressions and lead to an enduring sense of personal guilt or a doubting of self-worth.

To confess one's sins is described in the *Catechism of the Catholic Church* as an admission of personal faults in order to gain forgiveness and a cleansing from all unrighteousness (#1847). Individual faults can be readily identified from an officially compiled schedule of sins that have been defined and graded according

---

[62] *The Modern Catholic Encyclopedia* (Dublin: Gill & Macmillan, 1994), p804.

to their deemed seriousness as an offence against God. Sins fall within two principal categories – 'mortal sin' and 'venial sin'. The former is judged to kill the life of the soul and leave the sinner without sanctifying grace and there is an obligation for Catholics to confess all mortal sins according to number and species. Venial sins are regarded as less serious but still carry a residual consequence, which must eventually be expunged.

To constitute mortal sin, the *Catechism* states that the incident has to involve 'Grave matter' and to be committed with full knowledge and deliberate consent (#1857). Grave matter is specified as being one of the 'Ten Commandments' listed in the *Old Testament*, and full knowledge and complete consent presupposes an actual knowledge of the sinful character of the act and its opposition to God's law. It also implies a consent that is sufficiently deliberate to be a personal choice (#1859).

As regards venial sins, these are considered to weaken charity and produce a disordered affection for created things and, if unrepented, 'can dispose us, little by little, towards committing mortal sin' (#1863). I remember the time when this resulted in regular prompts from the pulpit during Sunday Mass to encourage fortnightly (in some cases, even weekly) personal confessions.

I am not questioning the merits of the Sacrament of Confession (or 'Reconciliation' as it is now more commonly referred to) but rather what, for my generation, could sometimes be regarded as a routine exercise by which to obtain absolutions without the need to reflect fully on the circumstances of the subject matter. The deemed certainty of being able to secure a 'quick fix' could therefore leave people ill-equipped to pursue a thoughtful and balanced adult Christian approach when faced with the need to resolve many of life's challenges, particularly those involving less-than-straightforward personal and family issues.

Generally speaking, people today have become more questioning and are less likely than previously to passively accept rules and regulations as binding 'under pain of sin', especially in the case of mortal sin with its stated consequence of eternal punishment. If people use the word sin, it needs to make sense to them in light of their personal experience without an undue legalism inherited from the past.

Original Sin

The story of our first parents' disobedience against God's instructions came early in our religious education programme (Gen 3:15) and this original sin committed by Adam and Eve ultimately developed into the concept of 'original sin', as a central topic of Catholic teaching. The *Catechism of the Catholic Church* states that the personal sin of Adam and Eve contaminated human nature, which they transmitted subsequently from what had become their 'fallen state', and as a result of our common lineage its consequences would be our unavoidable inheritance. For us, it is a sin that is 'contracted' not 'committed'; it is a 'state' not an 'act' (#404).

In searching for sources to support this teaching, the *Old Testament* describes a sequence of events that took place in the Garden of Eden and makes frequent reference to the sinfulness of humanity and our need for salvation, but I cannot find any explicit reference to a primeval sin that was to be passed on to future generations. In the *New Testament*, St Paul speaks of the universality of sin, which he describes as a condition of human nature, something inside each of us that is in conflict with our inner being and can cause us to do things we really hate (Rom 7:15).

It could perhaps be argued that the strong emphasis on sin by St Paul (more than sixty individual references in his writings) may have led later theology to read Genesis as a literal description of sin. Under this scenario, our parents could be thought of as being created in grace and endowed with preternatural gifts (i.e. beyond what is normally found in nature), such as clarity of mind, strength of will and freedom from pain , but all of this became forfeited by their act of disobedience.

The *Catechism* then recites a list of ensuing consequences: Adam and Eve lose the grace of original holiness; they become afraid of the God of whom they have conceived a distorted image – that of a God jealous of His prerogatives; their harmony is destroyed; the control of the soul's spiritual faculties over the body is shattered; the union of man and woman becomes subject to tensions; harmony with creation is broken and visible creation becomes alien and hostile. Death makes its entry into human history (#399/400).

I find this a depressingly negative tirade and the immediate question it raises for me is: why would God create humankind in a particular form, knowing full well that in short order we would fail to meet His expectations and from that point onwards we would never again reflect His originally intended blueprint? Moreover, the term *original sin,* as an attempt to describe our human condition, was not coined until the early 5th century when it was used by St Augustine in his defence of orthodox Christianity.

In this regard, it is important to consider the message that St Augustine intended to convey at the time with his use of Greek phraseology. The generally assumed verdict is that original sin is in the nature of a generic condition, which is passed on through successive generations and which we automatically inherit as a result of being descendants of Adam. However, an equally valid explanation could be that the term is simply meant to describe the similarity between us and Adam whenever we are tempted to commit our own particular misdemeanours. It will be apparent that there is a fundamental difference between these two interpretations.

Formal Church teaching on *Original Sin* dates from the Council of Trent in the 16th century, so whatever one's personal opinion there is no way of avoiding such a declared finding. However, as with all official pronouncements, they are a product of the culture and theology of the time and if one distinguishes between the substance of the teachings and the formulations that were considered appropriate to meet the then prevailing circumstances, it would seem, in the words of *The Modern Catholic Encyclopedia*, that (i) Jesus Christ is at the very centre of the divine plan; (ii) all human beings have a basic need for the redemption he brought about; (iii) this need is antecedent to any act of sin on their part or even mere exposure to a sinful environment.

I believe this is a closer fit to St Paul's comments regarding the universality of sin and following this line of thought, modern biblical theology offers the view that Chapter 3 of Genesis is not telling us about what happened at the beginning of human history, but is a story of what is happening all of the time. Instead of describing a historical first sinful act, it presents an ingeniously simple picture of what every sin really is, namely the human self-assertion of those who want to think of themselves as God and who want to go their own way in deciding what is right and wrong.

The Garden of Eden might therefore be seen as a picture of how God would like us to be: in harmony with ourselves and the surrounding world; not ashamed of being fully known because we have nothing to hide; and always enjoying an intimacy with Him. Effectively, the exact same elements as those referred to in the above 'litany of woes' but now expressed in a positive rather than a negative fashion. In this way, the human story can begin not with sin but with God's intimate love, which we can never lose and from which it might be said that sin is something that happens along the way – in a sense, it is to be expected statistically.

Under this arrangement, the faith core of the doctrine of *original sin* is that without grace, no human can rise to the level of existence that God planned for us. In becoming fully human like us, Jesus is the proof that God's grace is an intrinsic element of our human make-up and that each of us came to be so that God can share his life in this way. What better explanation than this can we expect to receive in order to describe the reason for our human presence?

Old Sins: New Sins

My *Penny Catechism* listed seven 'Capital' sins or vices, so named because they were regarded as the source from which all other sins take their rise. These were accompanied by a further six sins, which had been specifically singled out as being against the Holy Spirit, together with an additional four sins that 'cry out to heaven for vengeance' (#324, 326, 327). There was certainly no shortage of sins in those days and we were advised in addition of ways in which we might cause or share in the guilt of another person's sins (#329).

The seven listed capital sins (sometimes referred to as The Deadly Sins) were accompanied by a list of 'complimentary virtues' (#325). Our lives involved a daily contest between:

Capital sins	Virtues
Pride	Humility
Covetousness	Liberality
Lust	Chastity
Anger	Meekness
Gluttony	Temperance
Envy	Brotherly Love
Sloth	Diligence

Looking back at this approach, the first column listing is automatically presumed to involve sin for which we need to identify an ameliorating virtue. What a different outlook on life we might generate if virtues were shown as the constitutive components of our 'graced' human existence, and the second list of corresponding sins are examples of how we can, on occasion, fall short of these ideals?

This same competing list of sins and virtues remains in force today, although I suspect that our understanding of a number of the individual words will have altered over the years. Collectively, they display what I would term a 'churchy ambience' and are likely to exert a diminishing influence outside this context. They also continue to be listed without any real pastoral guidance to help form a subjective judgement. For example, when does working towards the financial security of oneself or one's family become covetousness? What is the dividing line between gluttony and temperance? How meek does meek have to be and do each of these apply in equal manner to every person in every situation?

Lists such as this were intended to help us measure our personal behaviour, but how to assess rights, wrongs and justice generally in civil affairs, politics or corporate business? Decisions in these spheres may well be taken for perfectly valid or economically sound reasons, but could still result in unintentional collateral consequences that affect the well-being of a broad range of people.

The social well-being of the community at large was a topic frequently raised by St John Paul II, who considered that decisions relating to the human environment could give rise to structures of sin that impede the full realisation of those who were oppressed by them. In his view, this called for courage to replace such structures with more authentic forms of living in community.[63] We might perhaps take heed of his advice and turn the searchlight towards some of the precepts relating to Church teachings and practices that continue to be enforced – however well intentioned the original motives may have been.

Scandal

The image at the base of the word 'scandal' is that of a snare or stumbling block that causes someone to falter. The most obvious example in a religious context is tempting another person to sin. St Luke records Jesus's warning that it would be better to be cast into the sea with a millstone around one's neck than to scandalise any of his followers (Lk 17:1).

But not all scandal should be avoided. Jesus knew that his preaching would be a stumbling block for many and he declared as blessed all those who would not be scandalised at him (Matt 17:1). St Paul continuously preached of Christ crucified even though this was an event that was regarded as a scandal by those seeking a glorious and powerful Messiah (1 Cor 1:23). It is possible to conclude from this that the former type

---

63 Pope John Paul II, *Centesimus Annus*, 1991.

of scandal should be avoided, but that we should be encouraged to exercise the latter by speaking and acting in the truth, even in the face of opposition.

The avoidance of scandal is treated as a high priority by the institutional Church in order to seek to preserve an unblemished corporate image. Whilst the views and actions of individual members of the faithful are often judged as a cause for scandal, the regular exercise of Ecclesial Authority seldom seems to be subjected to the same level of scrutiny. One wonders how many people may have left the Church or been dissuaded from joining because of the views of individual theologians compared with the numbers who have been adversely affected or discouraged by a perceived lack of pastoral sensitivity and support at parish level?

The most extreme example of institutional action to avoid scandal has been the handling of the clerical sex abuse incidents over many decades. The betrayal of trust in this manner by those involved is extremely disturbing, but to allow this to continue under a veil of secrecy and subterfuge at the highest levels of the Church is quite appalling. How could we have so lost sight of Jesus's example to ever imagine that this could be an acceptable way in which to behave?

The scars that have resulted from these actions will take a long time to heal, but for some people in the Church, this is an episode they now tend to regard as past history. I am not sure that the issue has yet been fully resolved and whilst I would not wish to perpetuate an ongoing inquest for longer than necessary, I fear that despite the safeguards now in place, there could still be future occurrences that receive like complicity and attempts at concealment. I sincerely hope that I am wrong, but under any similar circumstances in the future, I believe it is the responsibility of every Catholic to purposely 'give scandal' by speaking and acting in truth whatever appeals there may be to notions of Church loyalty.

In summary, I consider that we have allowed the concept of sin to dominate the Catholic agenda to an unhealthy degree. I am not disputing the existence of sin or doubting its debilitating consequences, but what I do question is our apparent preoccupation with the subject and the wholly negative outlook that can follow as a result.

Our faith tells us that Jesus conquered sin and death so that we might have life to the full (John 10:10). Surely this must be our starting point and primary focus of attention. We are not immune from sin and evil, but we should not act as if we are hostage to its presence. We are born into a world of bacteria that continuously surrounds us and to which we sometimes fall prey, but if we allow this vulnerability to dominate our daily lives we would soon become raging hypochondriacs.

In a religious context, I believe this is what many Catholics are prone to be and often with unfortunate results in terms of a diminished view of self-worth and an accompanying sense of fear and despair. For others, the perceived odds of being able to avoid all incidents of sin are viewed as being far too long to even warrant the attempt.

On a more positive front, there is an emerging realisation that moral theology and pastoral practice has, up until now, been excessively 'act-orientated' and modern clinical research has begun to focus more on 'person-centred' criteria. That in order to know how a person stands in terms of moral questions, more is required than simply a check of individual acts. For mortal sin in particular, it is no longer considered sufficient to determine a situation by a purely objective measurement of a material action in isolation. An act may be bad or evil in the abstract, but it cannot be labelled a moral evil or sin until the whole person is considered in the context of understanding, intentions, foreseen possible consequences and all the other circumstances that are required to assess moral responsibility.

I believe there is a serious need for us to examine our present 'house view' and overall approach towards sin. The aim should be to establish an adult understanding of what constitutes sin, the range of circumstances and subjective ingredients that might apply and the choice of pastoral remedies that can be adopted.

Our considerations must be anchored on Jesus and the *New Testament* as the unchanging indicators of God's love and compassion, but should also incorporate the fruits of modern scholarship in the field of human sciences – the study and interpretation of the experiences, the activities and the constructs associated with human beings. Our primary purpose is not to indict or to condemn, but to provide the reassurance of God's understanding and unshakable love of all that comprises the human condition.

THE CATHOLIC CHURCH

Contemporary wisdom would have us believe that the answer to every question can be found through *Google*. A search under the heading 'The Catholic Church' will therefore indicate the following:

> 'The oldest continuously functioning institution in the world: a religious organisation which is led by the Pope, who as Bishop of Rome is considered by Catholics to be the successor of St Peter; the office of the Pope is called the papacy and his ecclesiastical jurisdiction is referred to as the Holy See – a recognised sovereign entity with which international diplomatic relations can be maintained.
>
> […] The Church's function is to spread the Gospel of Jesus Christ, administer the sacraments and exercise charity. The sacraments are efficacious signs of grace instituted by Jesus

Christ and entrusted by him to the Church to aid the spiritual growth of its members. Catholic beliefs are summarised in the Nicene Creed and detailed in the *Catechism of the Catholic Church*. These beliefs are based on Scripture and Tradition and are collectively referred to as the 'Deposit of Faith'.

[…] The Deposit of Faith continues to be interpreted by the Church's teaching authority ('magisterium') which has been divinely bestowed on the Pope and his fellow bishops. Solemn definitions concerning matters of faith and morals are guided by the Holy Spirit and in specific circumstances they are deemed to be infallible.'

As far as it goes, there is nothing untoward in any of this and I imagine it represents a description that most Catholics are likely to recognise and accept. But does it really explain what the Church is and how each of us relate to it?

The Second Vatican Council was convened to consider questions of this nature and with the benefit of sixty years' subsequent pastoral experience, I propose to revisit and comment on the bishop's findings under five headings: the nature of the Church; ministry in the Church; authority in the Church; the papacy; and the *sensus fidei*.

The Nature of the Church

The unequivocal view that emerged from the Council is that the Church is something that is alive within us. It is not simply a structure that has been planned and constructed and which exists over and against us (*Lumen Gentium* #2). We ourselves are the Church; we are an organism of the Holy Spirit. We go on living, developing and adapting, as does every other living thing, and yet in essence we are always the same because Jesus is forever present in people's hearts and it is from people's hearts that Jesus shapes the Church – not the other way round.[64]

To refer again to the opening sequence of *Lumen Gentium*, Jesus is 'the light of the world' and our role is to mirror his glory and reflect his radiance. In order to achieve this, we are baptised and become incorporated into his body – we are 'the Body of Christ' of which he is the head and each of us has our place as one of its visible organs. Together, we comprise a community that takes its form in a life of prayer, a life of the sacraments and in our fundamental attitudes of faith, hope and charity.

With the assurance of Jesus's continuing presence, we are a body that grows from the inside outwards in that our faith acts as an encouragement for others to join us and for them to similarly experience hope and love. The Church is described as a Sacrament, an

---

[64] Joseph Ratzinger, *The Ecclesiology of Vatican II* (Faith and Politics, 1988), p5.

outward sign of inward grace, which makes us at one and the same time a spiritual community and a visible society, an earthly Church and a Church endowed with heavenly riches, and these combine to form a single complex reality that is centred on Jesus (LG #8).

We are an entity that lives and grows as a result of our continuing relationship with the objective person of Jesus at a point in history and the subjective experience of the presence of Jesus throughout our 'Spirit-led' history. This calls for us to maintain a balance between these two dimensions, as if we overemphasise the objective there is the risk of us continually living in the past and emphasising features such as centralism, legalism and conformity. An overemphasis of the subjective can lead to excess individualism without foundation or structure.

These were differing notions of 'Church', which were examined by the 19th-century German theologian Johann *Möhler* (1796–1838), who saw the former as being very much the Catholic position in which the scope for the individual was limited to obedience under authority. The latter was seen to reflect more closely many of the Protestant Churches, where teachings and institutions only came to life when they were expressions of the interior belief of each contemporary community.[65]

---

[65] Philip J Rosato, 'Between Christocentrism and Pneumatocentrism' in *Heythrop Journal* 19, 1978, pp46–70.

In *Möhler*'s view, neither of these alternatives was acceptable. His solution was to regard the Church as a visible community of believers founded by Jesus in a body that is now his extension in time and space, and within which the divine and the human operate concurrently, in that it is not possible to have one without the other. Effectively, *Möhler* uses the doctrine of the 'hypostatic union' of the two natures of Jesus (see Council of Chalcedon, page 11) as an analogy to explain the Church as Jesus made visible in us as the continuation of his incarnation.[66]

Later in the same century, Saint John Henry Newman (1801–90) emphasised that baptism was more than merely a symbolic sign of belonging to the Church, as through our anointing we each become recipients of the triple office of Jesus, namely that of priest, prophet and king. This takes its origins from the *Old Testament* where priests were understood as mediators or a bridge between God and humankind, prophets were regarded as witnesses to truth in word and deed, and kings were seen as providing leadership along the right path.

These several insights of *Möhler* and Newman found their way into *Lumen Gentium* and served to expand our understanding of the true nature and purpose of the Church and our role within it. That rather

---

[66] Peter Riga, 'The Ecclesiology of Johann Adam *Möhler*' in *Theological Studies* 22, 1961, pp563–87.

than thinking of ourselves as members of a religious institution, we should come to appreciate that we are the live component parts that collectively make up the institution that is the Body of Christ.

A key feature of *Lumen Gentium* is the centrality of the Eucharist in God's plan. At the 'Last Supper' between Jesus and his closest disciples, he introduced them to a liturgy of his death and resurrection and gave them the feast of life. In doing so, he recapitulated the earlier covenant that had been given on Sinai but this time in a real rather than a symbolic fashion, by establishing a community of blood and life between God and humankind. It is the Eucharist that links men and women not only to each other but also with Jesus and in this way it turns people into the Church.

Lumen Gentium goes on to emphasise that the Church of Jesus is really present in all legitimately organised groups of his followers and it is these individual communities that collectively constitute the 'One, Holy, Catholic and Apostolic Church' (LG #26). In other words, each 'Eucharistic Community' is already completely the Church because each community possesses Jesus completely. The caveat 'legitimately organised' is included to ensure that each community is in union with its pastors. A group of people cannot simply meet, read the scriptures and claim to be a Church on the grounds of Jesus being present when two or more come together in his name.

As regards the pastors, they are stated to fulfil their roles not as individuals but in conjunction with one another and by working as a group towards the larger unity of the Church. They are members of a particular community that can trace its origins back to the original 'Twelve' who were appointed by Jesus. This concept of 'Collegiality' is therefore of the essence of the office of a bishop and can only be lived and put into effect in such a community context. And as Vatican II makes abundantly clear, it is a community that is always in union with the 'Roman Pontiff' as the successor in title to St Peter (LG #22).

The document then introduces the concept of 'the People of God', which is a further term that can be found in the *Old Testament* and in Christian terms denotes a chosen people to include all who accept the crucified and risen body of Christ and who seek to live in relation to him. In the words of St Peter (1 Peter 2:9–10), this makes them 'a chosen race, a royal priesthood, a holy nation, a people for his possession… who in times past were not a people but now are the people of God' (LG #9).

It is a concept that acts also as an 'ecumenical bridge', when addressing the issue of those outside the legal unity of the Catholic Church. Thus, it is possible for non-Catholic Christians to be classified as 'being joined in many ways' and non-Christians spoken of as being 'related' with all of us being called to be pilgrims (another term taken from the scriptures) and serving to emphasise that the Church has not yet reached its final goal. Its own hope is still ahead of it.

Lumen Gentium concludes with a chapter on Mary, the Mother of God. A number of the bishops considered this to be a subject that should be dealt with in a separate document, but by agreeing to Mary entering directly into the doctrine on the Church, it reinforces the opening assertion that the Church is not some piece of machinery or institution, or even one of the usual sociological entities. It is a person. It is a woman. It is a mother. It is living.

This Marian understanding of the Church has been described by the late Emeritus Pope Benedict XVI as:

> 'the most decisive contrast to a purely organisational or bureaucratic concept of the Church. We cannot make the Church: we have to be it. And it is only to the extent that faith moulds our being beyond any question of making that we *are* the Church. The Church is in us and it is only in being Marian that we become the Church. In its origins the Church was not made but born. It was born when the intention 'Let it be to me according to your word' awoke in the soul of Mary. The deepest desire of the Council was that the Church

should awaken in our souls. Mary shows us the way.'[67]

In light of these several insights, I regard Vatican II as being in the nature of a new Pentecost in which the Spirit was at work to help us equip ourselves for the task of evangelisation in a rapidly changing world. Our original mandate from Jesus did not include an itemised operating manual, simply a promise of continued guidance and support by his Spirit. With Jesus as our point of reference, our priority is to work with the Spirit in order to be as sure as we ever can be at any one time of what we are presenting and to ensure that our witness is compatible with what we profess.

In terms of continuity in the Spirit, we should count ourselves as privileged in being the present living example of the 'Body of Christ' for our own times. This is a role that must surely rank as a joy rather than an imposition or a burden, and is one that generates an enthusiasm for each of us to continue to proclaim the 'Good News' in a manner suited to present circumstances.

Ministry in the Church

Jesus interpreted his life and work as a service for the sake of others and called on us to follow suit. Ministry

---

[67] Joseph Ratzinger, *The Ecclesiology of Vatican II* (Faith and Politics, 1988), p20.

is therefore an intrinsic component of being a follower of Jesus and as this is described by St Paul: '...There are a variety of gifts but the same spirit, and there are varieties of service (ministries) but the same Lord and there are a variety of workings but it is the same God who inspires them all in everyone' (1 Cor 12:3–6).

In practice, Catholics generally tend to associate ministry with the ordained priesthood and the hierarchical structure within which it operates. There has been a wider use of the term since Vatican II, but most lay ministries still tend to be regarded as subsets of the ordained priesthood, which is often portrayed as representing the exact model of Church that Jesus intended.

As a result, we have allowed our common fellowship in Jesus through baptism to develop into a two-tier system that emphasises the distinction between the ordained and the non-ordained. This is further compounded by the former exercising complete and unquestionable control over all facets of theology, liturgy and administration, as well as operating in accordance with their own internal processes.

The word to describe this is 'clericalism'. It is a subject I believe calls for an urgent and frank discussion if the Church is to make progress in a new era of its history. In my view, this should begin with an honest re-examination of basic principles: what were Jesus's intentions for ministry in his Church; how did this develop into the structures of authority and priesthood that exist today; and are there other initiatives that we might examine to help meet future pastoral needs?

The example of Jesus
Jesus chose to be born into the tribe of Judah, '…the members of which have never done service at the altar… everyone knows he came from the tribe that Moses did not even mention when dealing with priests' (Hebr 7:13–14). By contrast, he could have chosen the tribe of Levi, which was traditionally associated with the priesthood and the Temple, by virtue of Jewish Law and physical descent.

The primary focus of Jesus's public activity was to announce the nearness of the Kingdom of God and to call people to repent and follow the Scriptures (Mark 1:14–15). It was a message that he delivered in person and often did so during visits to synagogues and the Temple precincts, but any association with the prevailing framework of worship and the sacred appeared to remain with him a chance one and presumably therefore of secondary importance.

As a result of the incarnation, we are able to consider ourselves as brothers and sisters of Jesus by adoption. It follows from this that each of us are co-joined with him in his approach and sacrifice, which makes us priests in our own right. Jesus is the mediator of a priesthood that is given to all who are addressed by God as sons (Heb 12:5–8) and all who love one another like brothers (Heb 13:1).

In Jesus, we have been granted a 'right of entry' to the Sanctuary that was previously reserved for official priests and each of us is able to offer worship in the form of our own lives that have been transformed from within by the communication of Jesus's life (Heb 10:19–25). The ministry of Jesus continues in the Eucharist as his bequest to us and comprises our guarantee of God's unshakable ongoing relationship with the whole of humanity.

The Apostolic Era
During the course of his public ministry, Jesus chose twelve men to become his closest collaborators. The number twelve signified the historic twelve tribes of Israel, and for the sake of the whole of the people of God, the 'Twelve' would become the foundation stones of a New Israel (Revelation 21:14). Their composition included fishermen, a former collaborator with the occupying power and a one-time terrorist, which is not perhaps the most obvious choice for leadership selection, but it does indicate the way Jesus intended to gather all parties and all mentalities to himself.

The Gospels refer to the twelve interchangeably as disciples and apostles, which I regard as an important reminder that they were disciples first and then apostles (i.e. sent forth). In other words, they were not an independently selected group who were handed responsibility for ministry, but drawn from among those who were already active followers of Jesus. Their future role would always remain secondary to their primary calling.

This was also a 'collective recruitment', which signified the creation of a new community in which each individual had significance not in his own right but because of being in union with Jesus and with the other members of the group. In similar fashion, the particular responsibility given to St Peter was an expression of his particular brief as a member of the twelve, not an independent role and function. Jesus chose twelve apostles to include Peter, not eleven apostles plus Peter.

The sending out of the twelve by Jesus was to follow the same pattern as his own, namely to proclaim that the kingdom of God was close at hand. There is no evidence that they were endowed with perfect knowledge or special insights and, like us, they would have been forced to live with the same questions and seeming contradictions of life with the need to rely on the support of the Spirit through whom we all, in our individual ways, continue to participate in the one priesthood of Jesus (LG #10).

The itinerant ministry of the apostles was successful in attracting new followers who formed Christian communities to celebrate the 'Word' and participate in the 'Supper of the Lord', always confident of the abiding presence of Jesus among them. The pattern that began to emerge was for individual Christian families in a particular location to issue a welcome and lay on the hospitality in their homes to accommodate an 'assembly' of fellow Christian neighbours. Clearly, the pastoral welcome was an important function in the service of the Church as this was what continually reformed the *Ecclesia* (the coming together of the followers of Jesus) whenever it gathered to hear the words of Scripture and renew the 'Lord's Supper'.[68]

An assembly in a domestic setting could also be seen and experienced as a part of the regular rhythm of people's weekly life. It was an ideal environment in which to form the 'communion' that was the local Church and to act as the leaven to attract interest from outside. The success of the local Church did, of course, depend upon the choice of people who would extend the welcome and preside over the assemblies, and these first 'shepherds' of the Church, the Elders (*presbyteroi*) and Supervisors (*episkopoi*) were selected from among those with a good reputation locally and, in particular, with an established record of successfully running their own households.[69]

During the early decades of the Church, there were two parallel forms of ministerial input: an itinerant ministry that followed the pattern set by the apostles and a growing residential or localised ministry to

---

68 Jean-Paul Audet, *Structures of Christian Priesthood* (Sheed & Ward, 1967), p24.
69 Ibid, p140.

serve the increasing number of individual Christian communities. In terms of the former, we learn from the *Didache*[70] that under the supervision of the apostles there were numbers of travelling prophets and teachers who made regular short-stay visits to individual Church communities in order to add support to the resident ministers and reinforce the message of Jesus.

It is apparent also that the apostles and their successors in both forms of ministry did not think of themselves, nor were they thought of by their respective communities, to be a 'sacral caste' in the same way as the Levitical priesthood. Numerous generations of the Church lived out their Christian inheritance based on the home and family without considering a need to extend the area of the sacred to their pastoral structures or bestow an inalienable character on the persons who had been chosen to perform the gestures or to preside over the rites.[71]

The early Church

By the end of the apostolic era, there was an expanding network of local Christian communities that were individually structured and run in a manner that suited their own particular circumstances. The only consistent characteristics were a sense of brotherhood

---

70 Also known as the 'Teaching of the Twelve Apostles' – a written compilation by an unknown author from the mid-2nd century, covering moral, liturgical and disciplinary issues.
71 Jean-Paul Audet, *Structures of Christian Priesthood* (Sheed & Ward, 1967), p128.

and brotherly love between the individual communities and a strong commitment at each local level to provide help and support for those in need.

The practical appeal of Christianity at that time was this visible living community dimension ('see how these Christians love one another'), together with the added attraction of functional simplicity compared to the sacral world of Judaism. These were the factors that made it possible for the primitive Church to break out from its Jewish roots and become a part of the vast Roman Empire. By lifting to some extent the burden of the sacred, the young Church gained enormous flexibility for its structures, functions and services, and these first communities were assured a wide freedom of action, invention and adaptation.[72]

With the passage of time, a more standardised structure began to take shape within each of the local communities. A distinction emerged between the previously interchangeable titles of *presbyteroi* and *episkopoi*, whereby the latter – which we now refer to as bishops – assumed a presidency of each local Church in place of the previous committee approach to pastoral leadership.

In view of the difference between the nature and function of an itinerant preacher and that of a resident minister, the role of bishop in today's Church could

---

72   Ibid, p128.

perhaps be said to have evolved from a presbyter by way of 'elevation' rather than from an apostle by way of 'localisation'. The claim that bishops are the direct successors of the apostles might possibly be more accurately expressed as heirs to the authority of the apostles rather than their specific apostolic function.

In any event, by the 4th century, a vertical or hierarchical structure had more or less become the norm in most Christian communities, comprising a bishop, presbyters and deacons. And as a result of their direct association with the Eucharist, bishops and presbyters increasingly began to be referred to using the Greek title of *Hiereus* (in Latin, *Sacerdos*) meaning priest. The sense of involvement with the sacred, which is suggested by the name, soon became extended to cover everything connected with their person and function, together with the objects used in the service of worship and the buildings used for the weekly community assemblies that had long since outgrown their original domestic bases.

History will attest that a dualism between the sacred and the profane had been endemic from time immemorial (*Gnosticism*), but this did not seemingly find a place in the pastoral consciousness of the early domestic Church. In the *New Testament*, the title 'priest' applied only to Jesus and it was to him and through him that a common priesthood was understood to have existed for the whole of the people of God by virtue of their baptism. Nowhere was the title priest ever used in reference to the *presbyteroi* or *episkopoi* and so this form of ministry, which looked to have severed its link with its Jewish predecessor, started to become similar to the model it had replaced with all of its accompanying sacral undertones.

The Constantine Factor
The ending of official persecution of Christians and a decriminalisation of Christian worship was assured by the 'Edict of Milan', which was ratified in 313 AD by the Emperor Constantine (AD 274–337). This was an event that produced far-reaching and enduring changes in the Church.

The immediate effect was a dramatic increase in Church membership as being a member of the State was effectively the same as being a member of the Church, but without the need to make the same conscious personal choice or commitment. The Church became seen as civil society in its religious aspect with bishops appointed to act as officials charged with responsibility for administering the spiritual agenda of the State.

In some quarters (to include the Emperor), this alignment of Church and State was promoted as the definitive coming of the Kingdom of God and from this emerged the concept of 'Christendom' as a geopolitical power, which would eventually reach its peak during the Medieval period. A further consequence of the direct association with the Empire was that the Church came to be seen as a single universal institution rather than a network of local Church communities bound together by a sense of fraternal commitment. With Rome as the capital of the Empire, the Church in Rome and everything associated with it also began to assume a primacy that went beyond its previously acknowledged pre-eminence as the place where St Peter and St Paul were martyred.

The Roman Empire and its political structures always paid serious attention to the concept of the 'sacred' and a strict demarcation was generally enforced between the perceived realms of the sacred and the profane. Everyday life was full of such boundaries and due ritual process was deemed necessary to pass between the two, providing obvious encouragement to those within the Church who favoured the re-emergence of a pronounced sacerdotal form of priesthood.[73]

One of the principal results of the growing emphasis on the sacred was that the earlier pastoral traditions of the Church, which had been concerned with the provision of service rather than the style of life of those connected with it, witnessed a reversal of priorities to the extent that the style of life itself became thought of as an appropriate 'state of life' with its own meaning and value. This state of life could therefore be idealised and,

---

73   Edmund Hill, *Ministry and Authority in the Catholic Church* (London: Geoffrey Chapman, 1988), p38.

as future history can attest, it progressively attracted more emphasis and attention for itself than the purpose for which it was intended. It was also an easy subject for Church authorities to issue ever stricter rules and regulations.[74]

The long-term effect of this change in outlook is that what started out as a common priesthood of the whole of the people of God – originally *laos*, meaning people without distinction – became divided into specific categories of clergy and laity. The former were associated with the sacred and the latter with the profane or matters to which the clergy were officially precluded.

A growing involvement by the bishops in the affairs of the State also gave rise to potential conflicts of interest in what had effectively become their twin functions. The need for the Church to remain free from secular interference placed added responsibilities on the bishops and often resulted in a need for them to accept accommodations and compromises that reflected conventional civil values and standards of behaviour.

Ministry today
Fast forward to the present time and we find ourselves as a Church with an estimated world membership of

---

74   Jean-Paul Audet, *Structures of Christian Priesthood* (Sheed & Ward, 1967), p141.

some 1.2 billion souls. In succession to St Peter, we have a Rome-based Pope and as heirs to the authority of the apostle there are some four thousand bishops worldwide, who are assisted by upwards of 400,000 ordained priests.

Entry to the priesthood is restricted to male Catholics who, with few exceptions, are unmarried and who are required to remain so. They will have completed an authorised programme of study and training, and their ordination into the priesthood confers the sacrament of 'Holy Orders', which is administered by a bishop to whom each 'ordinand' is incardinated (enlisted).

The role of a bishop is to act as 'Vicar of Christ' in the local Church of which he is appointed to be its principal pastor and under the guidance of the Spirit he is responsible for preaching the gospel and ensuring that the Eucharist is offered as the means by which the Church continues to live and grow (LG #25/26). As a member of the episcopal college with the Roman Pontiff as its head, each bishop is called to be solicitous for the entire Church, with an obligation to foster and safeguard the unity of faith and to uphold the discipline that is common to the whole Church (LG #23).

The role of the ordained priest is to assist his bishop in ministering to the needs of the local faithful to whom he is assigned. His lifestyle and behaviour is regulated by the 1983 Code of Canon Law with a principal obligation for celibacy, a requirement to offer the Eucharist and carry out the liturgy of the hours, make spiritual retreats and frequent approaches to the sacrament of penance (#276). Priests themselves are bound together in a sacramental brotherhood and under their bishop they form a priestly college within each diocese.

The Second Vatican Council reintroduced the ancient office of 'deacon', whose function was to assist both the bishops (*episkopoi*) and the elders (*presbyteroi*) by fulfilling a range of pastoral responsibilities. Today's ministry of 'Permanent Deacon' means that there is no automatic progression to the ordained priesthood and whilst the position is currently restricted to male Catholics, married male candidates are able to apply.

An ordained priest becomes eligible at a future date to be appointed a bishop, which is an office that is deemed to convey 'the fullness' of the Sacrament of Holy Orders. Since the beginning of the 20th century, virtually all bishops have been selected and appointed under the auspices of the Pope through a process of selection and recommendation involving papal nuncios (ambassadors) who reside in each country of origin. As the sole prerogative of the Pope, individual bishops can be further promoted to become cardinals in order to assist him in the running of the universal Church. On promotion, each new cardinal becomes the 'titular' parish priest of a nominated parish in the diocese of Rome and is thereby entitled to participate in the election of his future diocesan bishop – namely the Pope. The papacy therefore sits astride the entire hierarchical apparatus of the Church.

The Church now operates as a single worldwide entity. Legislative and administrative control is in the hands of the Pope and his Curia (his purposely selected Rome-based bureaucracy) with day-to-day instructions delegated to individual bishops for them to implement in their respective territories. Ministry has become aligned with authority and is exercised within a chain of command, which is reserved primarily for the ordained and applied in strict conformity to officially approved ecclesiastical policy guidelines.

Whilst accepting the need for structures within an organisation of our size and geographical diversity, I consider that the present 'Roman System' has, by virtue of its nature and composition, resulted in a ministry that is increasingly narrow in outlook, legalistic in approach and bureaucratic in application. Despite the earlier mentioned provisions in *Lumen Gentium*, concerning the status of each of the local Churches, they are effectively treated as if they are individual operating units that form part of a single worldwide 'Corporate Entity'. An entity in which it might be possible to visualise Jesus as 'Life President', the Pope as 'CEO', the Curia as 'Executive Directors' and the rest of the bishops as 'Regional Managers'.

We are currently suffering from a serious fall in active Church membership and there is a continuing shortage of new recruits for the priesthood, but despite this our pastoral leadership appears determined to continue to operate as if nothing needs to change. It is a view that is frequently accompanied by the claim that our present structures and approach to ministry reflects a divine blueprint that is not ours to challenge. It will be evident even from this brief outline of ministry that such a claim is simply untrue.

One is forced to conclude that our pastoral leadership regard the preservation of their ministerial status and its control over the entire range of Church practices to be as important as providing for the spiritual and sacramental life of those for whom they are responsible. As a result, there are growing numbers of the faithful for whom it is increasingly difficult to access the Eucharist and other Sacraments because of the shortage of ordained ministers; a shortage that is based on present canonical definitions and qualifications relating to ministry.

One location where this situation has been an acute problem for many years is the Amazonian Region in South America, and this prompted Pope Francis to convene a Bishop's Synod in 2019 to examine the case for boosting the number of priests by ordaining married men and allowing women to become deacons. Citing the Vatican II Decree on the Ministry and Life of Priests (*Presbyterorum Ordinis*), which had stated that celibacy is not demanded by the very nature of the priesthood

(PO #16), the 184 voting bishops who attended the Synod (mostly from the nine countries that contain a share of the Amazon rainforest) produced a cautious approval for a) married priests; b) women deacons; and c) the establishment of an Amazonian Liturgical Rite.

However, Synods in their present constituted form are merely advisory forums and the final judgement rests with the Pope. There are rumours that Pope Francis is not wholly in favour of married priests at this point in time and for women to become deacons it is alleged that a recasting of traditional Church teaching could be a necessary precondition. Under these circumstances, it seems unlikely that there will be a positive response any time soon to address these present difficulties.

In my view, to purposely delay or to avoid coming to terms with prevailing shortages of ordained ministers in the Amazonian Region or anywhere else makes a mockery of the findings of the Vatican II document on the Sacred Liturgy – that the Eucharist is '…the summit to which the activity of the Church is directed and the source from which all its power flows' (SC #10).

Vatican II upheld the view that legitimate diversity among local Churches did not historically harm the communion and unity of the universal Church, but rather expressed and served it – a view supported by the plurality of rites and disciplines that exist today throughout the Church (see LG #13 and The Decree on

Catholic Eastern Churches (*Orientalium Ecclesiorum*)).

The example of Jesus in respect of ministry is as real for us today as it was at the time of his earthly presence. It requires a response that is sympathetic to the needs of our own times and is expressed in a manner that reflects the social and cultural fabric of each local Church. We should not consider ourselves to be forever fettered by past decisions on individual roles and responsibilities that might once have been considered appropriate to meet the then prevailing circumstances.

Authority in the Church

Authority can be defined as holding the power to give orders and to enforce them; to lay down the law with the expectation of compliance; to wield influence; to control; to rule; to guide effectively. This highlights the distinction between authority and ministry if we accept the real meaning of the latter, namely to serve or carry out commands or to act as an instrument through which the possessor of authority is able to exercise influence or to control or rule.

What Jesus proposed was 'ministerial authority', which at first sight might appear to be a contradiction in terms. For this not to be the case, it becomes necessary to either recast the concept of authority or allow the idea of ministry or service to evaporate. There is little doubt in my mind which of these options was intended by Jesus. For him, authority was only for the sake of service.

This is a view supported by several texts from the Gospels such as the response Jesus gave to James that '...whoever must be great among you must be your servant, and again, whoever would be first should be the slave of all' (Mark 10:42–45). We might also include: 'He who is the greatest among you shall be your servant and whoever exalts himself shall be humbled' (Matt 23:8–12).

How then to reconcile these two seemingly conflicting concepts? The Latin word for authority is *potestas,* which is a legal or juridical term and was the word that was almost always adopted to translate the originally used Greek word *excousia.* A further examination of the Greek indicates several variants that stem from its root source and which for our purpose might be considered to most closely resemble what we would now refer to as a 'licence'. Authority understood in this sense could therefore be taken to mean a right or an entitlement; to have authority to do something; a freedom of action that is capable of being enjoyed by those under authority, as well as those exercising it.

In other words, there is greater scope to interpret the word 'authority' in Greek; in particular to have *authority* is to have *liberty,* and conversely to have *liberty* is to experience *authority.* Unfortunately, history records that this wider interpretation of the word authority became rather short-lived in the Latin (Roman) Church, where its understanding and application soon reverted to a more military form of usage.

Aside from the way in which the concept of authority is to be understood, it becomes important also to consider where authority in the Church is vested and the manner in which it is intended to be exercised. The general perception today is that authority is vested with the Pope and his bishops, with a qualified level of delegation to ordained pastors at individual parish level. In his book, *Ministry and Authority in the Catholic Church,* Edmund Hill contrasts the authority we should reserve for God and Jesus with that which Jesus bestowed on the Church as a whole, on the apostles as part of that whole and on St Peter as an individual.

This makes it clear that the fullness of authority (*plena potestas*) rests with Jesus alone as head of the Church, but that this authority, like the other privileges and titles of Jesus, is participated in by all members of the Church. This means that the entire body of the Church shares in the *plena potestas* of Jesus. It is derived 'directly' from him as a result of baptism, faith and commitment. It is in no sense abrogated by, or dependent upon, other participations.[75]

The *plena potestas* of the apostles and, in turn, today's bishops is also derived immediately from Jesus

---

75 Ibid, p19.

by virtue of their role, which is to be at the service of the local and universal Church. Likewise, St Peter and his successor Popes enjoy this same fullness of authority as a result of being the focal point of unity for all of the communities in all of the local Churches.

There is no evidence that Jesus laid down a definitive schedule of how these three 'funds of *plena*' should be coordinated, but giving full value to each of them would certainly be congenial to the overall sentiment that is conveyed by the readings in the *New Testament*. In practice, the power wielded by the possessors of the three funds has grown or shrunk during the course of the Church's history in proportion to the degree of structural institutionalism each has managed to establish, and which has usually been achieved by one at the expense of the others.

The essential message of the *New Testament* is that all of the baptised constitute a family in which God is our Father, Jesus our elder brother and the Spirit our continuing guide. As a family, we are directed towards ministering to one another and each of us is called to contribute our own particular talents to support the common objective of proclaiming our given family values to the whole of humanity. The area of contention today is the manner in which responsibility for family duties has become allocated, codified and is required to operate in practice. It has created demarcations that challenge our inner unity by allowing what I would describe as 'class distinctions' to gain citizenship. I believe this is illustrated in three current features of Church life:

Priest and priesthood
The word 'priest' can be traced to two sources. First, as a translation of the Greek *hiereus* (Latin *sacerdotos*), meaning a person who is endowed with sacred powers and duties, especially the power to offer sacrifices to God. Secondly, it can be understood as the shortened version in English of an attempt to pronounce the Greek word *presbyteroi,* as the collective name given to the chosen community leaders in the early Church. Thus, we now use a word that can describe two distinctive roles and functions; a confusion that did not exist in the *New Testament* or in the early Church where the title of priest was reserved exclusively for Jesus, with 'priesthood' being a term that applied to everyone who had been baptised.

A common priesthood of the baptised was reconfirmed by Vatican II, which referred to our consecration as a spiritual house, and that by persevering in prayer and praise we should present ourselves as a sacrifice, living, holy and pleasing to God, and give reason to everyone for them to hope of eternal life (LG #10). This same clause went on to state that '*though they differ essentially and not only in degree* (my emphasis) the common priesthood of the faithful and the ministerial or hierarchical priesthood are nonetheless interrelated and each in their own way share in the one priesthood of Christ.'

I find the above wording to be a little confusing. The clause could simply have said that the common priesthood of the faithful and the formally ordained members of the Church are ordered to one another and each in our own way share in the one priesthood of Jesus. I am not a Latin scholar, but I am reliably advised that the English translation of the Council text gives greater prominence than the original Latin to what appears to be the above purposeful additional words and prompts me to ask: a) if there is an 'essential difference' within the common priesthood, then what is it? and b) within a single shared priesthood, how is it possible to hold an essential difference in common?

As for ordination to the priesthood, I attended a ceremony recently in which the candidate was described as being ordained to 'the Sacred Priesthood'. This was followed by a prayer that referred to his forthcoming office as a 'Priesthood in the Presbyteral Order' – which are two terms that once again refer to two different functions. Perhaps the intention is to boost the provenance of the former by an implied historical association with the latter.

At a personal level, Catholics have tended to create a mystique relating to the office of priest – that in some way he is 'taken up' to a separate or higher level. The letter to the Hebrews (5:1) is often cited in support of this with the result that the sacred is assumed to have been 'assigned' to clerics and is identified with actions that are reserved solely to them, with the secular pertaining to the laity or actions forbidden to clerics.

However, as *Lumen Gentium* makes clear, those who receive the Sacrament of Holy Orders find their priesthood given a character that distinguishes it from the priesthood of others as a result of the responsibilities it places upon them as part of God's ongoing plan of salvation – not by any superimposed philosophical or sociological categories.[76] Moreover, if we are to integrate our faith into our lives, we need to avoid a constant 'dualism' between the sacred and the secular as, without exception, we live in a world that is both sacred and secular. This was recognised by Pope Paul VI when he spoke of the Church having an authentic secular dimension, and that it was because of this that we are able to fulfil our role of offering life to the whole of creation.[77]

I remember being on a pilgrimage some years ago at the Marian Shrine at Walsingham in Norfolk, and having arrived in good time, I was able to observe the arrival of the coaches bringing pilgrims from different parishes within the diocese. What was noticeable was that on leaving the coaches, the priests and people

---

76 Michael Richards, *A People of Priests: The Ministry of the Catholic Church* (Darton, Longman & Todd, 1995), p55.
77 Geoffrey Robinson, *Confronting Power and Sex in the Catholic Church* (The Columba Press, 2007), p28.

who had travelled together as one group immediately went their separate ways; the priests to join their fellow clergy and the rest to form a separate group as the congregation. Rightly or wrongly, this struck me as a divisive feature in what had begun as a single shared community endeavour.

As regards the actual ceremony of ordination, we talk of a person being ordained and receiving the Sacrament of Holy Orders, but what is involved here? The word 'ordination' comes from the Latin *ordines,* meaning to arrange or to put in order and was the language of Roman law, which classified society into various *ordines* or orders. The word 'ordo' later became used as the formal description of the sacrament of Orders or ordination, and so properly speaking it could be taken to mean that it is the Church that is ordained through one of its members being placed in a certain position within it. The ordination of a bishop or priest does not arrange them in isolation, but in relation to others and to other groups of people.

Holy Orders was formally pronounced as a Sacrament of the Church at the Second Council of Lyons (1274), with the 'holy' appendage being a predictable consequence of the sacral mindset that had developed in the Church in relation to those who were directly associated with the Eucharist. By definition, a sacrament is '…an outward sign of inward grace ordained by Jesus Christ, by which grace is given to our souls' (*Penny Catechism*, #249), although unlike the rest of the sacraments, Holy Orders is not conferred purely for the benefit of the 'ordinand', but for the well-being of his ministerial appointment and the community which will be served by it.

Hierarchy
The word does not appear in the *New Testament*, which is not in itself an issue, but does perhaps suggest a need for caution with its use and application. It derives from yet another Greek source and refers to the control or management of sacred things, which makes it easy to see how and why it emerged to describe those associated with the dispensing of the Eucharist.

The Catholic tradition has been to treat the hierarchy as extended holders of the promise Jesus gave to the apostles that 'whoever hears you hears me' (Luke 10:11) and 'as the Father sends me, so I send you' (John 20;20), and this continues to colour people's attitude towards episcopal authority in general. Vatican II described the Church as 'Hierarchical' (i.e. the actual title of Chapter Three in *Lumen Gentium*) and this might therefore be taken to imply that differences in status are constitutive of the organisation. A proposition I find difficult to reconcile with what I regard as the unambiguous approach to equality, ministry and brotherhood enunciated throughout the *New Testament*.

Our current hierarchical Church structure can be said to date mainly from the 4th-century 'makeover' by Constantine and has frequently been prone to wrangles over the ordering or importance of particular Churches (Rome, Constantinople, Antioch, Alexandria) and between the holders of individual offices carrying titles such as Archbishop, Metropolitan and Patriarch as a means of denoting seniority (superiority?). In today's speech, the word hierarchy implies a ranking or a chain of command, which, in a Church context, might, in the extreme, be taken to imply that the higher one's position is in the ecclesial hierarchy, the closer one is to God. Could this perhaps explain the increasing use of the title 'Holy Father' when referring to the Pope?

Careerism is a feature of any human-run organisation, but the Church only exists to adhere to a specific vision of the world centred on Jesus, which should preclude the same kind of emulous competition that might be acceptable in a secular context. The members of the Church, to include the highest office holders, are merely trustees of the deposit of faith we have received through Jesus and our collective duty is to improve our understanding of what we have been given in order to faithfully transmit this to successive generations.

An obvious feature of our present hierarchical structure is that it is reserved exclusively for those who are ordained and over the centuries it has developed its own protocol for self-perpetuation. This is the 'Roman System', which carries with it a deemed sacred mantle for all office holders and frequently seems to exclude them from the levels of accountability that their individual and collective behaviour might otherwise warrant. As a purely minor example of this tendency, I remember, many years ago at school, being forcibly told that 'if I could not think of something nice to say about a priest, I should refrain from saying anything'.

The Roman System also creates an environment in which it is difficult for those in a position of authority to ever feel able to admit to past mistakes or to readily contemplate change in case this might imply being wrong previously. The inevitable result is a collective inertia, which is strongly geared towards preserving the *status quo* – at all costs.

An alternative view proposed by Hans Kung, who was yet another of the *periti* at the Council was that:

> 'The promise of Jesus Christ was not that the Church will never make mistakes, but that it will survive its mistakes, for the truth of Jesus Christ will always be present in the Church, tarnished and even obscured, but always there to be rediscovered. The promise is that in spite of many errors in detail, the Church will be maintained in the basic truth of the Great Tradition – the continuing process of handing on from generation to generation – and that the

ugliness in the Church will never completely destroy its underlying beauty. The Church's faith will often be weak, its love lukewarm, its hope wavering, but that on which its faith is based, its love rooted and its hope is built will always endure.'[78]

Magisterium
This is a word which, in my view, has become a 'catch-all' term for the purpose of Church governance. The word itself originates from the Latin *magister* meaning a master in a particular field of activity and in our context it is generally taken to mean 'teacher'. It is a term that has become concretised to apply to those who exercise a teaching role in the Church, namely the Pope and the bishops.

It is frequently used with a prefix such as 'sacred' or 'authentic', presumably with the intention of boosting the importance of whatever is being said or written. It is sometimes alluded to also as if it exists as a 'reservoir of wisdom', which is owned exclusively by the hierarchy to enable them to deal with all things religious.

As it is described in the Vatican II Dogmatic Constitution on Divine Revelation (*Dei Verbum*):

> 'The task of giving an authentic interpretation of the word of God whether in its written form

---

[78] Referred to by Geoffrey Robinson, *Confronting Power and Sex in the Catholic Church* (The Columba Press, 2007), p260.

or in the form of tradition has been entrusted to the living teaching office of the Church alone. Its authority is exercised in the name of Jesus Christ. This magisterium is not superior to the word of God but is rather its servant. It teaches only what has been handed to it. At the divine command and with the help of the Holy Spirit it listens to this devoutly, guards it reverently and expounds it faithfully. All that it proposes for belief as being divinely revealed it draws from this sole deposit of faith' (DV #10).

I have purposely quoted the clause in full in order to emphasise that the magisterium is not simply *carte blanche* for any opinion that may be expressed from time to time by those in authority. This was made clear in the caution expressed in St Matthew's Gospel of not treating anyone as a master other than Jesus (Mat 23:10), and years later St Augustine expressed his own anxiety at being called upon to be a teacher and which he then proceeded to qualify with a number of pertinent observations.

In the first place, Augustine considered it the responsibility of bishops and people to help each other when attempting to learn from Jesus as the one true master. Secondly, that the obligation of a bishop to teach should take the form of a dialogue between teacher and pupil in which the latter is not expected to be a passive recipient, but is called to exercise a critical judgement on what is being said or written. Thirdly, there is the need for constant vigilance by the teacher to avoid 'slipping up' on what is actually said and finally, there is a continuing requirement for prayers and critical sympathy from the faithful.[79]

Contrast a more recent opinion expressed by the 20th-century Pope Benedict XV (1914–1922), '…all know to whom the *magisterium ecclesia* has been given by God; to this one therefore belongs the complete right to speak as he thinks fit when he will; the duty of the rest is religiously to comply with the speaker and to be hearers of what is said.'[80] More recently, Vatican II called for a religious docility of the will and the intellect to be extended in a special way to the authentic teaching authority of the Roman Pontiff and to teaching formally proclaimed by bishops who maintain a bond of communion with him (LG #25).

The question is: what constitutes 'authentic teaching'? Without a clear definition, it becomes possible for all manner of teachings to be fused by association with the 'infallible magisterium' of the Pope. Whilst the latter has been defined (*Pastor Aeturnus*, from Vatican I), I consider that it is poorly understood both inside and outside the Church, and this can lead some people to regard every papal

---

79 Referred to by Edmund Hill, *Ministry and Authority in the Catholic Church* (London: Geoffrey Chapman, 1988), p75–77.
80 Ibid, p78.

pronouncement as oracular ('creeping infallibility') and to apply an almost similar stamp of approval on routine teachings of individual bishops ('gradual infallibility').

As a formal theological definition, the word 'magisterium' is a comparatively recent introduction and I believe there is a need to examine its use in the context of the Church in which the Spirit has incorporated every believer and given him and her a special role in building up the body of Christ (1Cor 12:4–11). This is the charism known as the *sensus fidei* – the sense of faith, which is considered in more detail below but which can be described briefly as the Holy Spirit at work in the hearts and minds of all who make up the Body of Christ in order for them to properly discern the truths of revelation in their own times.

Vatican II urged the laity to make themselves heard by expressing their needs and wishes with confidence. As stated in *Lumen Gentium,* 'In proportion to the knowledge, the competence and the distinction which they enjoy, they have the right (*facultas*) and sometimes even the duty of expressing their opinion on matters affecting the good of the Church' (LG #37).

The text went on to say that these opinions should be progressed through the institutions established by the Church for this purpose and always with '…truth, frankness and prudence, as well as with respect and love towards those who by virtue of their sacred office represent Christ'. The only difficulty with this was that when the Council came to a close, there were no such obvious institutions in existence and, to my knowledge, this is a situation that is not significantly different today. Not a particularly respectful and loving reciprocity towards the laity.

What is also noticeable today is the extensive use of an upper case 'M' when referring to the magisterium as if the intention is to preclude any further discussion on a particular topic. In my view, this represents an uncalled for and dispiriting feature of authority, which not only serves to emphasise the distinction between the hierarchy and the rest of the Church, but can also lead to divisions within the hierarchy itself. One such example was the post-Vatican II controversy between the Vatican and the bishops of South America in relation to so-called 'Liberation Theology'.[81] This resulted in one set of theologians being condemned and outlawed by another set of theologians, who were by no means endowed with greater theological acumen or greater fidelity to the whole Catholic tradition. It was just that the latter set happened to be Rome-based.

A further concern relating to the magisterium is that whilst Vatican II referred to a submission of the

---

81   A 20th-century theological method in opposition to earlier intellectualism and fideism in the Church, which introduced a wider social dimension for Christian action to counter criticism from social/political commentators such as Kant and Marx.

will and then the intellect to the teaching authority of the Pope (LG #25), more recent edicts from Rome have reversed the order and now propose a submission of the intellect and the will (see Canon Law #752). The implication here is a required automatic intellectual consent, rather than this being based on the regard and acceptance of the position of the person who is teaching. As this is described by Bishop Geoffrey Robinson, 'It is the difference between a willingness to accept the Pope as a teacher and automatic acceptance of every word the Pope uses.'[82]

And so despite the clear affirmation by Vatican II on the transcendent character of one's personal conscience, there appears to be an attempt to use the 'Sacred Magisterium' to secure unquestionable conformity to all teaching as the litmus test of orthodoxy and loyalty. In my opinion, this is a far from encouraging scenario and signals a need for the whole subject of the Church's teaching authority to be a high priority for serious prayer and equally serious re-examination.

We need to find and maintain an equilibrium in teaching that provides positive guidance without excess rigidity and avoids treating every question that is raised as a potential act of dissent that needs to be stamped out. We will do well to heed the advice from Gabriel Daley that the Gospel we profess to seek and to serve

---

82   Geoffrey Robinson, *Confronting Power and Sex in the Catholic Church* (The Columba Press, 2007), p121.

demands honesty, freedom and love in the way in which we practise, teach and explore it.[83]

As a summary, ministry in the Church is a constituent element of Christianity, which involves the whole of the people of God. Jesus indicated the form of ministry he was seeking, namely one of service and persuasion rather than domination and coercion, and he appointed twelve apostles to oversee the task. Their appointment came with an assurance of his continued guidance, leaving them to decide how best to develop and implement their pastoral responsibilities and to determine their individual and collective roles in consultation with the communities they were to serve.

Over the ensuing centuries, the theology of ministry has become distorted by an exaggerated and almost exclusive focus on the concept of an ordained priesthood. A priesthood that sacralises those who are ordained and, by implication, desacralises the remainder of the faithful. It has resulted in ministry becoming a facet of authority and Church governance and is retained as the sole preserve of one component of the people of God. The overall result is an introspective organisation that is frequently viewed as being synonymous with the hierarchy, that is inclined to treat itself as the goal of its own strivings, and sees its principal objective as being to defend and preserve particular ritual or worship

---

83 Gabriel Daley, 'Faith and Theology' in *The Tablet*, April 1981, p446.

systems, which are deemed to be essential for purpose in their precise current form.

This all said, it would be uncharitable to conclude any consideration of ministry in the Church without emphasising the debt of gratitude owed to the unsung legions of pastors and religious who have faithfully fulfilled their ministerial vocation over the years – and indeed who continue to do so. They will know who they are and they will be able to witness the fruits of their labours by the affection this continues to generate among their people. They can be confident that they will forever remain as beneficiaries of our prayers.

To leave the last word on the subject to Bishop Butler:

> 'There must not be a conflict between authority and freedom in which one side can only win at the expense of the other. Rather, there should be a dialogue of which the ultimate resolution is always left to conscience. Human responsible freedom to which the faith itself makes its appeal is the supreme value which the Church subserves.'[84]

The Papacy

There is a presumption, if not an insistence, that on all matters of importance, Catholics must first look to

---

84 Christopher Butler, *In the Light of the Council* (Darton, Longman & Todd, 1969), p103.

the Pope for direction and guidance. It is the Pope who decides what is and what is not important, and with our present system of Church Governance, it is the Pope alone who has authority to make changes.

The starting point for the papacy was the call by Jesus for St Peter to be 'the rock' upon which he would build his Church (Matt 16:17–20). From this beginning, we are able to point to a continuous line of succession up to the present time, with our own Pope Francis (1936–) as the 266th recognised heir to the authority of St Peter.

The role Jesus conferred on St Peter can be seen to be specific but, as mentioned previously, it was contained within the same framework as the appointment of the other apostles. I interpret Peter's title of 'Rock' as being, for him, to act as a solid foundation, and therefore a point of reference and a symbol of unity for his fellow appointees. A view supported by the promise of Jesus to pray that his (Peter's) faith would not fail and that he would then strengthen his brothers (Luke 23:31–32).

In our own time, the late Emeritus Pope Benedict XVI described the primacy of St Peter (and, in turn, each of his successors in authority) as not being in opposition to the collegial character of the Church, but understood as a primacy of communion in the midst of the Church, living as a community and understanding itself as such. It means the faculty and the right to decide authoritatively within the network of communication where the 'Word' is being witnessed correctly and consequently where there is true communion. It presupposes the *communion ecclesiarum* and can be understood correctly only in reference to it.[85]

Even with a specifically endowed faculty, it is evident that St Peter was not free from criticism by his fellow apostles and was always accountable for his actions. We read in Acts that he encountered opposing views at the Council of Jerusalem and he is later reported to have been severely censored over his decision to eat a meal with a non-Jew on the grounds that this was against the law (Acts 10:1–48).

In terms of a connection with Rome, the City was the Imperial Capital of the Empire and therefore an obvious location for St Peter to visit in order to spread the message of Jesus. It was also the place where both he and St Paul were eventually martyred, making it a pilgrimage destination for Christians to visit and venerate their remains. Because of this connection, I suspect that St Peter is frequently assumed to have been the first Bishop of Rome and it is from here that the line of succession began.

In reality, there is no historical mention of a bishop or even the office of bishop for the Church of Rome prior to the middle of the 2nd century – anything up to eighty years following St Peter's death. Prior to this,

---

[85] Joseph Ratzinger, 'The Pastoral implications of Episcopal Collegiality' in *Concilium*, vol 1 (Glen Rock, NJ: Paulist, 1964), p25.

the Church in Rome probably had a governing body of elders (*presbyteroi/ episkopoi*) in the same way as most other Christian communities until customs changed and authority was conferred on a single life president or bishop.

The initial reverence towards Rome as a pilgrimage destination continued to grow over time to include its bishop (once it had acquired one), but it would be premature to speak of these early bishops as 'Popes', other than in the sense of being a father to the people in the local community, which would have been a title that applied equally to all other bishops. It was only in the centuries following the intervention of the Emperor Constantine that papal authority began to be extended, institutionalised and then justified theologically.

A theology of the Papacy was most clearly expressed by Pope Leo the Great (440–461), whose letters and sermons elaborated the traditional reverence towards Rome into the doctrine that every Bishop of Rome was the successor or heir to St Peter. Thus, a primacy of the Roman Church was turned into a primacy of the bishop of that Church and many centuries later this would be formally declared as such at the First Vatican Council (see again *Pastor Aeturnus*, p29).

Although Leo and his immediate successors would insist that they enjoyed the fullness of authority received immediately from Jesus through St Peter, it would not have occurred to them that this meant it was their duty and prime responsibility to govern the whole Church or even to think of the Church as a single universal entity. The Church was made up of local Churches, which were the responsibility of each resident bishop who would typically liaise with his fellow bishops by means of local or regional synods. The Bishop of Rome would simply exercise what might be described as 'a watching brief'.

At the end of the first millennium of Christianity, the brotherly fellowship between the individual Churches had broken down with the Churches in the East and West going their separate ways. Notwithstanding this, the Bishops of Rome continued to claim a universal sovereignty over all of the Churches and sought to expand the influence of the office in both civil and political arenas throughout Western Europe. As described previously, there were attempts to restrain papal ambitions by introducing a Parliamentary or Conciliar form of Church governance to which individual Popes would be accountable, but such proposals proved to be unsuccessful.

The Protestant Reformation in the 16th century challenged elements of traditional Church doctrine and also Papal autonomy, and this was followed in turn by challenges from groups of powerful European monarchs seeking to secure individual 'Royal Rights' over the Churches in their dominions. The 18th century saw the emergence of the 'Enlightenment' with its change of attitude towards intellectual thought and which sought to incorporate ideals such as liberty, progress, toleration, Constitutional Government and a separation of Church and State.

This movement was viewed by the Church as a threat to religion, and in order to contest what was perceived to be an increasingly secular outlook in society and a growing number of overtly secular States, a counter-movement developed in the Church across Northern Europe, which became known as 'Ultramontanism'. The title translates as being 'beyond the mountains' and refers to what is beyond the Alps, namely Rome and the Papacy. It was a movement that identified the Church exclusively with the Papacy and held that only a strong papacy could protect the Church and society in general from oppressive civil law-making and from heterodox ideologies.

At its most extreme, Ultramontanism was (and continues to be) a movement that supports the notion of 'papal absolutism' in all matters. Although not actually underwritten dogmatically, it is a concept that could be said to sit comfortably alongside the formal definitions of Papal Primacy and Papal Infallibility, promulgated by Vatican I.

Cause and effect
This, then, is our present-day papal inheritance. We have a Papacy with an unquestionable biblical provenance as the principal focus of unity in the Church, but

which has subsequently acquired or had thrust upon it presumptions of authority that reflect the model of an 'Absolute Monarchy'. We have a Pope who, as Bishop of Rome, is the head of a Sovereign State with his own appointed Civil Service; is the supreme legislator in matters of faith (infallibility) and discipline (Canon Law); who determines the nature and availability of the 'company product' and is responsible for hiring and firing middle-management (bishops).[86] One wonders how St Peter might have responded if he had been told that this would be his intended function?

The initial authority Jesus bestowed on St Peter was not accompanied by a detailed job specification, which makes it important for us today to reflect on both the possession of authority and the actual exercise of authority. For example, the Popes of the first few centuries will have possessed exactly the same 'fullness of authority' as 20th-century Popes, such as Pius XI, Pius XII, Benedict XVI and our present Pope Francis, but they did not (and indeed could not) exercise it in anything like the same way or to the same extent as at present. It follows therefore that if the total concentration of authority has not been wielded in the same way by every Pope from St Peter onwards, it is dishonest to promote the often heard view that the present nature and function of the Papal Office is of its

---

86 Eamon Duffy, *Faith of our Fathers* (Continuum, 2004), p61.

essence, and that it has always been so and is therefore not for us to question.

An example of the concentrated exercise of papal authority is the present procedure for selecting new bishops. This is initiated by Rome through its network of nuncios who investigate potential candidates in their respective countries and submit a shortlist for the Pope to reach a final decision. The Pope is under no obligation to accept a candidate from the shortlist and is entitled to make his own selection. It is a process that is all to do with control and conformity and it can create the impression that the whole of the world is the Pope's own diocese and each new bishop is appointed to act as his local representative. It is an arrangement that has an advantage of efficiency and convenience, but with it is the risk that the choice of candidates can reflect the particular mindset of those in a position of influence in Rome rather than in response to the immediate priorities and needs of each local Church.

The appointment of new cardinals to assist with the running of the Church is a further example of concentrated papal authority. The individual selections are the sole prerogative of the Pope and his choice of candidates will inevitably reflect some degree of like-mindedness towards existing papal policy. So, for example, there are currently 132 Cardinals who are eligible to select the next Pope, of which eighty-three have been appointed by Pope Francis.

In my view, we are witnessing an exaggerated form of Petrine Ministry. It is a role that has developed to support the view that the papacy is entirely independent of (and ultimately superior to) any other form of human authority. An authority that embraces all aspects of life and which, by its nature, is beyond human criticism and subject only to divine judgement.

In the minds of some of the laity, it is a claim that from time to time can become extended to include the whole Order of Bishops. In practice, however, their original 'apostolic authority' has become a pale wraith of its former self, as despite references to 'Collegiality' in the *New Testament* and its reaffirmation by Vatican II, this continues to be a concept that is mentioned more than it is actually seen to be exercised. And as for the original notion of an ecclesial authority that comprised the whole of the baptised, this has long since disappeared without trace.

We need to exercise continual vigilance to ensure that an essential unity is preserved in respect of Church teachings and practices, but we must have regard to the methods adopted to achieve this. The idea that there should be an unquestioning acceptance and conformity to every proposition simply because it emanates from Rome is not the 'charitable' solution we require. More to the point, it is not what I believe Jesus intended for his Church and it is a situation that can give rise to what Geoffrey Robinson has identified as 'the Five Vicious Circles':

1. The more the Pope insists on authority rather than persuasion, the less people listen, causing the Pope to feel the need to insist on authority.
2. The more a Pope insists on intellectual consent, the less people are willing to accept him as teacher, causing the Pope to insist on intellectual assent to what is being taught.
3. The more insistence there is on authority, the more faith will be presented as an intellectual assent to a series of propositions, and cause people to turn away from such propositions towards a religion of love and relationships.
4. The more people emphasise the importance of 'the individual' and the right to reach individual opinions, the more the Pope will stress the community nature of religion and this in turn will cause people to demand a more participatory community in which their opinions are listened to and taken into account.
5. The more people seek a voice in the affairs of the Church, the more the Pope can tend to turn towards a small group of loyal advisors rather than seeking the faith of the Church as a whole, and as a result create an even louder public clamour.[87]

---

87 Geoffrey Robinson, *Confronting Power and Sex in the Catholic Church* (The Columba Press, 2007), p124.

I consider that we are presently at 'Stage 5' and the challenge for us today is to determine how we interpret Jesus's intentions when he gifted 'authority' to St Peter as the rock upon which his Church would prevail. Was this an authority to single-handedly command, govern and control, or was it an authority to lead by means of service and example? I believe it is clear which of these Jesus intended, and the form this should take was well understood by Pope Gregory I (AD 540–604), who referred to himself as 'the servant of the servants of God' (*servus servorium Dei*).

An alternative approach
Against this background, I believe we could profitably return to and re-examine the nature and workings of the Petrine office during the early years of the Church. I am confident that this will point us towards the idea of separating the appointed successors to the authority of St Peter from what we currently refer to as 'The Papacy' or 'The Holy See', as a juridical office of corporate governance.

In other words, to return the Petrine office to being a pastoral function, which, under the guidance of the Spirit, acts as our source and assurance of unity, absent the whole gamut of subsequent legislative, administrative and political accoutrements that have attached themselves to the function. It is an arrangement that could still accommodate the referral of unresolved local Church issues to Rome in the cause of unity (a practice that can be traced back to the 3rd century), in contrast to our present practice of treating Rome as the sole authorised instigator for all Church business as well as judge and jury for every outstanding religious issue.

In terms of Church Governance, individual bishops could again assume full responsibility for the pastoral care of their local Church as well as accepting a shared responsibility for the well-being of the universal Church. This could be achieved by converting Bishops Synods from being purely 'consultative bodies', as at present, to become genuine 'deliberative and legislative bodies'. In this way, the Church can benefit from the collective pastoral experiences of active diocesan bishops rather than their deliberations being confined to purposely tailored agendas produced by a Rome-based coterie of administrative bishops.

A feature of the early Church was the flexibility for each local assembly to adapt itself to meet prevailing circumstances and this was achieved without detriment to the overall communion that existed among all of the Churches. I see no reason why a similar degree of latitude should not be afforded to today's Regional and National Conferences of bishops. This is not simply a call for independence but for a proper exercise of yet another long-established (and neglected!) feature of Church teaching known as 'subsidiarity'. That matters should be handled by the smallest and least centralised competent organisation to undertake the task rather than always being taken over by larger organisational structures or higher centralised authorities.

The application of 'subsidiarity' was re-emphasised by Vatican II, but in Church terms it remains another provision of the Council that has yet to be fully implemented. All the more surprising, perhaps, considering that Pope Pius XI (1922–1939) had previously stated in his 1931 Encyclical, *Quadragesimo Anno* (On the Reconstruction of the Social Order), that 'it was a grave evil and a disturbance of right order to assign to a greater and higher association what a lesser and subordinate organisation can do'.

As regards the Curia, I believe that consideration could be given to changing its present legislative, administrative and executive status in order to become a consultative body that is permanently at the service of the Pope and the college of bishops. Given the cumulative experience that exists within the various departments of the Curia, I would regard them as an ideal resource to continue to research, coordinate and communicate the fruits of the Church's Great Tradition for our collective benefit.

I consider also that the existing Rome-controlled process for the selection and appointment of bishops warrants further thought, prayer and consultation to better respond to prevailing pastoral priorities and sensitivities around the world. This, in turn, highlights the need for an improved regular dialogue between bishops, priests and people at each diocesan level along the lines indicated centuries ago by St Augustine. This will be achieved when everyone in the Church community considers themselves to have a part to play and a contribution to make. To quote the ancient Roman principle, 'What affects everyone should be discussed and approved by all'.[88]

It is evident that Jesus wished his Church to have Peter. We continue to need Peter in order to signify and exemplify our continuity with the past and, under the guidance of the Spirit, to be our symbol and assurance of unity for the future. The wearing of the 'papal tiara' as a symbol of earthly power has now been confined to history, but I consider that there are other elements of current papal protocol that call for further prayer and contemporary reflection.

We have the means to communicate and promote common objectives on a global basis, but the Christian message concerning Jesus can sometimes seem disjointed or even divisive. I consider that the office of the Bishop of Rome is where a Spirit-led initiative for unity should begin in order to lead us to proclaim Jesus with a single voice.

---

88 'Quod omnes tangit ab omnibus tractari et approbari debet'.

The Sensus Fidei

Vatican II gave prominence to the concept of the *sensus fidei* – the sense of faith that exists within the Church. It is a concept that is steeped in Scripture and Tradition and which holds that '…the Spirit of truth which comes from the Father and bears witness to the Son (Jn 15:26) enables all of the Baptised to participate in the prophetic office of Jesus as our faithful and true witness' (Rev 3:14).

As this is described in *Lumen Gentium,* 'The whole body of the faithful who have received an anointing which comes from the holy one (Jn 2:20 and 27) cannot be mistaken in belief. It shows this characteristic through the entire people's supernatural sense of the faith, when from bishop to the last of the faithful it manifests a universal consensus in matters of faith and morals' (LG #12).

What this is saying is that all of the faithful have an instinct for the truth of the Gospel by virtue of their baptism and this enables them to recognise and endorse authentic Christian Doctrine and practices and reject what is false. It is linked directly to the gift of 'baptismal faith' that each of us has received and is in stark contrast to the often expressed view that we comprise a 'teaching Church' (*ecclesia docens*), which is the exclusive province of the hierarchy, and a 'listening Church' (*ecclesia discens*), in which the rest of us are located.

So far so good, but the same text from *Lumen Gentium* then goes on to state '…by this sense of the faith, aroused and sustained by the Spirit of Truth, the people of God, guided by the sacred magisterium, which it faithfully obeys, receives not the word of humans but truly the Word of God' (see 1 Tm 2:13). It is reassuring to be told that we are in possession of the word of God, but the unqualified reference to 'the magisterium' does introduce an element of confusion in terms of which should come first. Is the role of the magisterium to pronounce from time to time on the expressed findings of the *sensus fidei*, or is it intended to dictate and determine the Church's entire ongoing process of discernment?

As matters currently stand, the assurance of truth within the Church is generally attributed to the exercise of the magisterium, which is expressed as being a 'gift' in the hands of the hierarchy. The term *sensus fidei* is not frequently mentioned in official communications and, among the faithful at large, it remains a relatively unknown aspect of Church teaching.

However, in 2014, the Congregation for the Doctrine of the Faith formally approved and published a document titled '*Sensus Fidei* in the Life of the Church'.[89] This was the result of a five-year study by the International Theological Commission (ITC),

---

89   www.vatican.va/roman_curia/congregations/cfaith/cti_documents/rc_cti_20140610_sensus-fidei_en.html

which comprised a body of thirty theologians from around the world who had been specifically appointed to examine the subject.

The ITC document provides a summary of the biblical, theological and historical background to the *sensus fidei,* together with an insightful commentary of how it can and should operate. How the whole of the faithful (and not forgetting that the clergy are also part of the faithful) are united in communion by the same Holy Spirit and actively bear witness to Jesus in their respective ways. No one in the Church is passive.

The document describes the *sensus fidei* as being composed of two distinct but related realities. The first comprises the Church in its entirety, which it refers to as 'the Church of the living God which upholds the truth and keeps it safe' (1 Tim 3:15). The second is each individual member of the Church who has become so by virtue of their baptism and reception of the Eucharist. The former is termed the *sensus fidei fidelium* and latter, the *sensus fidei fidelis.* A convergence (consensus) between the two is therefore the sure criterion to determine whether a particular teaching or practice genuinely belongs to the apostolic faith.

It then goes on to state that in matters of faith, all of the baptised have a right to be heard, and their reaction to what is being presented must be taken seriously because it is by the Church as a whole that the apostolic faith is borne in the power of the Spirit. Moreover, the *sensus fidei* needs to be understood not just reactively, as a means by which the faithful recognise God's truth when it is preached to them, but proactively in enabling them to probe and understand the Gospel that lives in their hearts and prompts their witness to it by word and action (#12).

Regarding the relationship between the *sensus fidei* and the magisterium, the document highlights two aspects. First, because all of the faithful are endowed by the Spirit with gifts for building up the Church and because all together are bearers of the apostolic faith, the magisterium 'has to be attentive to the *sensus fidelium* as the living voice of the people of God – it does not have sole responsibility for this' (#74). But, by virtue of their particular gift and calling in the midst of the Church, the Pope and the bishops are rightly seen to nurture, educate, discern and judge with authority the authenticity of the *fidelium* in seeking to ensure that opinions present among the faithful remain in accord with the Apostolic Tradition (#76–77).

It is acknowledged that there will be occasions when the reception of magisterial teaching meets with difficulties among the faithful and the document calls for appropriate action by both sides. The faithful must reflect on the teaching and make every effort to understand and accept it; resistance as a matter of principle is incompatible with authentic *sensus fidei*. The magisterium must likewise reflect on the teachings and decide whether they need clarification or reformation in order to communicate the intended message more accurately and effectively. These mutual efforts in times of difficulty express a communion that is essential to the life of the Church and a yearning for the grace of the Spirit to continue to guide us into all truth (#80, c/f Jn 16:13).

The relationship between the *sensus fidei* and theology is again stated to be twofold. It is seen first of all as a locus for theology; theologians depend upon the *sensus fidelium* because the faith that theology studies lives in the people of God. Secondly, the role of theologians is to serve the *sensus fidelium* by proposing criteria for its discernment (such as the production of the ITC document) and by assisting the faithful to know, understand and apply their faith (#81–84).

The document then turns to the differences and distinctions that need to be maintained between the *sensus fidei* and what might simply be expressions of popular opinion, particular interests or a reflection of the spirit of the age (#87), and it identifies a series of dispositions needed by members of the faithful in order to participate in the communion of the Church and thereby in the *sensus fidei*. These include a person's level of participation in the liturgy, mission and service of the Church, attentiveness to the Word of God, openness to reason as a partner to faith and a willing attentiveness to the teaching of the magisterium (#80–105).

The *sensus fidei* must, nevertheless, be understood as a theological reality. A reality that is intimately related to the gift of faith and to the life of the Church as a mystery of the communion that received its constitution from Jesus (# 113–114). Lay voices are to be respected and the history of the Church is shown to bear witness to times when it was the laity rather than the bishops or theologians who persevered with their view of faith (#119).

As described by St John Henry Newman, 'The body of the faithful is one of the witnesses to the fact of the tradition of revealed doctrine through the centuries'. It is therefore right and proper that our pastoral leadership should 'consult' the faithful in the sense of enquiring as to their actual belief(s) and take appropriate steps to ensure that this remains a living and lively process (#125–126). Such an exchange of views should be a prime means by which to gauge the health of the *sensus fidelium* and to identify what structures for consultation may be appropriate in order for the Church to remain 'living, lively and relevant'.

The implementation of the *sensus fidei* is what Pope Francis has described as one of the 'new ways' to assist the journey of faith of the pilgrim Church in helping us to recognise opportunities for both the planning and the content of future programmes for evangelisation. In order for this to be effective, bishops, priests and people must strive to remain in continuous close contact and dialogue with each other in order to determine the direction that we should follow to better respond to prevailing circumstances (#127). A policy that mirrors the advice given all those centuries ago by Saint Augustine (see page 197).

The document itself has been called a vital resource for the Church. An essential component that Jesus intended for us in order to help us determine our approach to evangelisation in each successive age.[90] As such, I consider that our pastoral leadership has a duty to provide a cohesive explanation of the nature and significance of the *sensus fidei*, and it would be helpful also if this was accompanied by practical examples that we could follow in our respective environments in order to make better use of our individual charisms in our 21st-century Church.

Can we expect to receive such a response? Based on the evidence to date of how Vatican II has been implemented, I remain ever hopeful without being over-optimistic. There could perhaps be an indication of what might be in prospect following the forthcoming Synod of Bishops later in 2023, for which the agenda is based on the findings of the recent questionnaire issued to the whole of the faithful to determine what being Catholic means to each individual. An agenda that on this occasion can therefore be said to represent the live, Spirit-led working of today's *sensus fidei*.

---

90   Paul McPartlan website, 'A vital resource for the Church'.

THE MASS

I made my first Holy Communion when I was seven years old. In those days we were 'prepared' for the Sacrament at school, which mainly involved memorising the relevant questions and answers in our *Penny Catechism*. I was taught that I would receive the Body, Blood, Soul and Divinity of Jesus, which was truly present under the appearance of bread and wine (#277), albeit in those days the laity were not permitted to receive the wine. It was explained that we were following the example of Jesus at his last meal with his disciples when he changed the bread and wine into his own body and blood, gave it to them to eat and drink, and asked them to continue to do this in his memory.

My First Holy Communion Mass and indeed every Mass was understood to be the same sacrifice as that of Jesus on the cross, which he continues to offer in an un-bloody manner on the altar through the ministry of his priests (#278). It is an offering to give supreme honour and glory to God, to thank him for His benefits, to satisfy Him for our sins and to obtain the grace of repentance, as well as all other graces and blessings through Jesus (#279).

Did I really understand what was involved here or how the change in the species came about? The answer on both counts was 'no', but I was prepared to accept the explanations I was given. After all, I had been called upon to believe that God had single-handedly created the universe and everything in it from nothing, so changing the substance of items of bread and wine seemed to be a comparatively minor undertaking.

Many decades later, I still attend Mass in memory of these events in Jesus's life, to which I include the memory of family and friends who have died (especially my parents and my granddaughter, Sophie) and I treat it as an occasion to offer my thoughts and my prayers for the well-being of my present family and friends. Along the way, I have also managed to uncover details of a number of events and practices from history that serve to prefigure the events of the Last Supper and add support to the belief that the 'Real Presence' of Jesus in the Mass is an intrinsic component of the entire creation narrative. Essentially, I remain satisfied as an adult with what I was initially taught when I was a child.

In terms of my investigations, the starting point was to give proper consideration to the times and the circumstances of Jesus's life. Jesus and his disciples were Jews, which made them part of a long history of a particular people's association with God and with God's law as understood and handed down through generations of prophets. Whatever was said and done by Jesus must therefore be viewed in a Jewish context.

A further consideration is the choice of vocabulary used in the Gospels and which began as a series of verbal testimonies that would have been spoken mainly in Hebrew with all the free varieties of expression this might entail. These accounts were eventually committed to writing but initially this was in Greek, which was subsequently translated into Latin and finally for our purposes into English. Imagine the task today of reporting the findings of Vatican II from just sixty years ago if all we had to work with were the latest versions of earlier notes and verbal accounts, and with few, if any, of the original participants still alive to corroborate the details.

To return to the 'Jewish dimension', the sharing of a meal had always been an important aspect of family and community life, with each meal expected to begin and end with a blessing in order to give thanks to God. This was accompanied by the breaking of bread and its distribution among those present to signify their unity as a group, in which each person would be conscious of eating a piece of bread taken from a single loaf.

The most important meal in the Jewish calendar was the feast of 'Unleavened Bread' which celebrated the

Pasch or *Passover* in remembrance of God's deliverance of Israel from their life of bondage in Egypt. The reference to unleavened bread can be traced back to an even earlier tradition which associated leaven with sin (particularly the sin of pride), and resulted in each family undertaking a scrupulous cleaning exercise every year to eliminate any trace of leaven from their homes. The call by Moses for people to prepare only unleavened bread for their journey out of Egypt can therefore be taken to mean that with God's help they were about to make a clean break with the past in order to start a new life. The feast of Unleavened Bread was stipulated to last for seven days.

Looking even further back into Jewish history there was a tradition among shepherds to sacrifice a young animal each springtime as a petition for the well-being of both shepherds and their flocks, and this included a smearing of the animal's blood on the entrance to their tents to ward off evil. This was later appropriated to interpret the deliverance of the Hebrew people from their bondage in Egypt when they were asked to sacrifice an unblemished lamb and paint their door posts with the blood to signify those who were to be delivered.

A further *Old Testament* thread is the understanding of 'memorial', which was not simply to recollect a past event, but by and through its celebration to make the event present and real. Thus, every time the Jewish

Passover is celebrated, the entirety of the episode connected with the Exodus story is made present in the memories of the people in order that they might continue to conform their lives to it.

So against this Jewish 'backcloth', what was Jesus proposing at the Last Supper? In respect of its timing, each of the gospels record that the event coincided with the annual Passover Feast of Unleavened Bread, which was offered as a thanksgiving (in Greek *eukaristein*, hence 'Eucharist') for Israel's liberation from slavery. The understanding of the Church has always been that each Mass is a thanksgiving to celebrate our liberation from the slavery of sin and which was achieved for all time by the one sacrifice of Jesus as our new unblemished 'pascal lamb'.

For the disciples, their participation in the traditional Jewish practice of the breaking of bread would have been confirmation of their unity with one another and especially with Jesus, and thereby made them co-participants in the whole movement of self-offering that he was about to make. From that point onwards, they would all remain firmly united and collectively comprise 'The Body of Christ', in which Jesus was its head and they its members.

The various Gospel accounts and writings of St Paul on the Last Supper can be seen to share a fidelity to the descriptive expressions used by Jesus but without a slavish literalness. He is not recorded as uttering exactly the same sequence of words in each case, as if these were intended to be some form of magical formula that should be repeated verbatim. His words expressed his overall intentions concerning the bread and wine and its connection with the events that would take place over the days to follow. His request for them to remember him was not just to recall these events, but to repeat them so that his sacrifice on the cross would be *represented* – 'made real' – at every Mass.

In this way, the bread and wine that had become the body and blood of Jesus would be the means of sustenance for our spiritual lives and serves to highlight yet another link with the *Old Testament*. This was the story of the Israelites who were physically sustained during their long journey out of slavery by 'manna' from Heaven, which was regularly and generously provided by God.

Just as an aside, what I do find surprising is the amount of coverage the authors of the Gospels considered appropriate to cover the Last Supper in view of its significance at the heart of the Christian Faith. For example, each of the Gospels of St Matthew, St Mark and St Luke devote no more than thirteen verses to cover the entire event. This compares with sixteen verses that St Matthew allocates to the parable of the labourers in the vineyard and twenty-one verses in St Luke to present the parable of the Prodigal Son. St John's Gospel is the longest account of the Last Supper but his focus is on the other event of the evening, namely Jesus washing the feet of the disciples, and contains no mention of the actual meal.

Also, there is no record of Jesus being asked to explain his intentions. This could suggest that the disciples were either dumbfounded by what they were hearing and seeing and did not know what to say or do, or they had an immediate grasp of Jesus's intentions as a result of their shared Jewish heritage. I suspect the answer will be more a case of the former, as to be told that what you were about to eat and drink was no longer what you had originally thought would surely have prompted at least one question. And as the crucifixion had not occurred, it would have been difficult for them to relate to the words of Jesus, which we now read of his body being 'given up' and his blood 'poured out', and they are hardly likely to have foreseen or even imagined the outcome to follow on Easter Sunday.

We are now called to come to terms with this same proposition that the bread and wine at Mass is changed into the body and blood of Jesus. In our contemporary language, to talk of bread becoming a person's body sounds incredulous and to speak of eating a person's body and drinking their blood repulsive, because they convey a particular meaning for us. This would, perhaps, have been less of a problem for the disciples at the time of the Last Supper as the Hebrew understanding of 'body' was not restricted to the physical or visible part of a person, but could relate more to what the person 'is'. In our vocabulary, this might be akin to include talking about an individual's personality.[91]

By the same token, the life of all creatures was seen in the *Old Testament* as being in the blood (Leviticus 17:11), and as life comes from God, blood was sacred, as the very symbol of life. As a consequence, it was permissible to eat the flesh of animals but not their blood, and blood shed from animal sacrifices in the Temple was taken to symbolise the self-offering of the person making the sacrifice – an act of dedicating their own lives to God.[92]

We now have the benefit of the Gospel narratives following the resurrection, which refer to Jesus 'touching' (Luke 24:39), 'eating' (Luke 24:41–43) and 'conversing' (John 21:15–22), which are all physical manifestations, but there are also references to Jesus's coming and going in a manner unlike a mortal body (Luke 24:31) or appearing in 'another form' (Mark 16:12). It becomes evident from these descriptions that the resurrection of Jesus should not simply be viewed as the resuscitation of a dead body.

St Paul highlighted a distinction between Jesus's physical body during his life and his spiritual body following his resurrection, but emphasised the continuity between the two – the person who was and

---

91 Paul McPartlan, *Eucharist: The Body of Christ* (Catholic Truth Society, 2004), p23.
92 Ibid, p24.

the person who will be (1 Cor 15, 35:49). The belief in the early Church was that Jesus did not return to his former manner of living after the resurrection, but entered into a new form of existence in which he shared his power with others. That the resurrection experience was not something that happened to Jesus alone, but something that can be shared by his followers. A new life for all in the power of the Holy Spirit.[93]

Given these several considerations, my take on the Last Supper is that the physical person of Jesus, who lived and had his being with the disciples, introduced them to the mystical Jesus he was about to become when he had fulfilled the mission to which he was committed. A glimpse of this mystical Jesus had already been given to a few of the disciples at the earlier episode of the 'Transfiguration' (Luke 9, 28:36), and through the breaking of bread he was now co-joining all of them as participants in his self-offering and making them sharers in the benefits that would ensue. Their unity with Jesus would endure forever and came with an assurance that his same '*persona*' would be present in a real and tangible manner in the bread and wine that future generations would offer when they came together in response to his instructions to 'do this as a memorial of me' (Lk 22:19).

This is an extraordinary claim by any standards and

---

[93] Robert A. Burns, *Roman Catholicism after Vatican II* (Georgetown University Press, 2001), p11.

one we can only speak of as being a 'mystery', which conveniently introduces us to another word that calls for a biblical explanation. For us today, a mystery is generally regarded as something that remains inexplicable, whereas in Scripture it can be used to refer to a plan or design that God intended for humanity and the world. As described by St Paul in his letter to the Ephesians, it is to sum all things up in Christ, to unite Jews and Gentiles through the cross so as to form a new person (Eph 1–3).

Predictably, there were mixed reactions among the followers of Jesus as events unfolded on the first Easter Sunday. Some people were unable or unwilling to accept the God-man dimension of Jesus, whereas others began, without difficulty, to pray to him. This is the choice we are now called upon to make. Do we believe in his 'Real Presence' in the Eucharist in which we are invited to partake or are we unable or unwilling to do so? Do we prepare ourselves to celebrate these Sacred Mysteries as we are asked at the beginning of each Mass and then collectively proclaim the Mystery of Faith following the elevation of the host, or do we simply repeat the words and pay lip service to their intended meaning?

The Body of Christ

This brings us to the Church's present teaching concerning the Eucharist and the use of the two descriptive expressions: 'The Body of Christ' and 'The Mystical Body of Christ'. The former is pronounced at Mass to accompany the offering of the consecrated host to which each communicant answers 'Amen'. The latter is generally used when referring to the Church. The point that needs to be made is that this is not how these expressions were used and understood in the Church during the first thousand years of its history.

The symbolism of sharing bread and wine as at the Last Supper will not have been lost on the disciples as a result of their common Jewish background and this was explicitly stated by St Paul when he spoke of our forming a single body because of partaking in the one loaf (1 Cor 10:6–17). It was even more forcibly endorsed in the 3rd century by St Cyprian who said:

> 'For when the Lord calls his body the bread which is made up of many grains joined together, he means by that the union of all Christian people which he contains within himself. And when he calls this blood the wine which is made into one drink of many grapes, he again means that the flock which we form is made up of individuals who have regained their unity.'[94]

The disciples at the Last Supper will have been conscious of Jesus's wish to become truly present in

---

94   Referred to by Henri de Lubac, *Catholicism: Christ and the Common Destiny of Man* (Ignatious Press, 1988), p90.

the elements of bread and wine, even though they were unlikely to have fully understood how and why. For them, the Eucharist would have been seen to comprise the mystical body of Christ, namely the body and blood of Jesus under the signs and symbols of the sacramental life he had introduced – in this case, in the form of bread and wine.

For St Augustine, Christ and the Church were inseparable and formed what he termed the *totus Christus* (the whole Christ), so to receive the body of Christ was to be received by him into his body, which is the Church. And as he famously expressed in one of his sermons, 'The Body of Christ you are told and you answer "Amen". Be members then of the body of Christ that your Amen may be true.'[95]

The unmistakeable testimony of the early Church therefore was that the Body of Christ was the Church, of which Jesus is head and we are its members, living out God's plan in unity with him and with each other. A family of local churches, a communion of communions until we all finally (and hopefully) become one Heavenly community. Meantime, the place where each of us most fully enters into this great historical plan is in the celebration of the Eucharist, or to again repeat the words of Henri de Lubac, 'The Eucharist makes the Church'.

---

95   Ibid, p92.

So why did a change come about in the use of these two expressions? The answer can be traced back to around the 12th century, when (not for the first time) doubts were expressed as to whether Jesus was really present in the sacramental form of bread and wine, and in order to eliminate any grounds for confusion or misunderstanding, the word 'mystical' was dropped from descriptions relating to the Eucharist. It reappeared some time later, but this time attached to the description of the Church.

The obvious next question is whether this reversal in terminology is a cause for concern? I believe the answer is 'yes' and this is explained by the 20th-century theologian, Paul McPartlan. In his words:

> 'Whereas the thoughts of the Fathers of the Church flowed naturally and smoothly from Jesus through the Eucharist to the Church (*Corpus Verum*), the train of thought now tended to stop short at the presence of Jesus in the Eucharist itself and the link between the Eucharist and the Church began to be neglected. What was now greatly studied was simply the way in which Jesus was present in the species of bread and wine.'[96]

An underlying belief in the 'real presence' had existed in the Church from the very outset, but around the

---

96 Paul McPartlan, *Eucharist: The Body of Christ* (Catholic Truth Society, 2004), p49.

same time as the change occurred in the use of the above descriptive terminology, theologians began to apply the word 'transubstantiation' as a means of explaining how the Eucharist could be said to have come about. Their approach was along the lines of Aristotelian logic concerning the basic distinction between a thing in itself, what it actually is (its substance) and what may be said about it in terms of quality or quantity (its accidents). Applied to the Eucharist, their interpretation was that Jesus actuated a complete change in the substance of the bread and wine, but preserved the accidents, which continued to taste, feel and smell like bread and wine.

Transubstantiation was adopted as an explanation for the Eucharist at the Fourth Lateran Council (1215) and shortly after, at the Council of Lyons (1274), the Eucharist became listed as just one of seven sacraments of the Church. I am not disputing the validity of these teachings or suggesting that transubstantiation represents a departure from what was the understanding of the early Church Fathers, but the change of emphasis in how to perceive the Eucharist prompted Henri de Lubac to comment that what had begun in the Church as 'a mystery to understand' had been turned into 'a miracle to believe'.[97]

One of the consequences of this change of perspective was that being confronted with a miracle of

---

97 Paul McPartlan, *The Sacrament of Salvation: An Introduction to Eucharistic Ecclesiology* (T&T Clark, 1995), p38.

this significance, many people considered themselves to be unworthy to receive the consecrated bread. To attend Mass and receive Holy Communion was no longer automatic and compelled the authorities to decree that the faithful should partake of the sacrament at least once a year, at or around Easter. The origin of what we still refer to as 'Easter Duties'.

To put 'transubstantiation' in context, it is a formulation not a definitive explanation of the Real Presence. The Council of Trent (1545–63) was very careful to point out that it represented a view that was 'not itself' part of the doctrine of the Real Presence, but merely an appropriate means by which to interpret the kind of change that the Church had always been proclaiming.

However, the real consequence of this change in terminology from these 13th-century Councils onwards has been for the Eucharist to no longer be seen as the 'encompassing orbit and dynamic centre of ecclesial existence', but simply one of several activities that form part of the Church's armoury. The Church had, in a sense, become a juridical institution in its own right and de Lubac's proposition that 'The Eucharist makes the Church' had, by default, become 'The Church makes the Eucharist' – and this could be thought of as an in-house product for the benefit of the faithful, which is made available by means of specific words and actions performed by an officially nominated celebrant as part of an approved liturgical rite.[98]

The Development of the Eucharistic Liturgy

Jesus chose twelve of his close disciples to join him at what would be their last meal together, but it is evident that they were not given a ready-made liturgy to follow. Their task then (and ours today) is to preserve the essentials of Jesus's mandate whilst giving suitable form and expression to its enactment in each ensuing age.

The history of the early Church shows that Jesus's followers continued to attend the weekly gatherings in the synagogues and participate in the readings and prayers. They then returned to the houses of fellow Christians in the vicinity to continue their own celebrations involving the breaking of the bread as Jesus had instructed. Several years later, Christians were barred from attending the synagogues, but because of the importance they attached to their scriptural heritage, they incorporated the readings from the Law and the Prophets into their own 'domestic liturgy' together with further readings based on accepted testimonies concerning Jesus.

From this point on, the weekly Christian Assembly comprised a 'Liturgy of the Word' and a 'Liturgy of

---

98   Ibid, p52.

the Eucharist'. The day on which the celebration took place was also changed from Saturday to Sunday to respect the day of Jesus's resurrection, and quoting from the writings of St Justin Martyr (died: 165 AD), the *Catechism of the Catholic Church* informs that:

> 'On the day we call the day of the sun, all of us who dwell in the city or country gather in the same place. The memoirs of the apostles and the writings of the prophets are read so much as time permits.
>
> When the reader has finished, he who presides over those gathered, admonishes and challenges them to imitate these beautiful things.
>
> Then all rise together and offer prayers for ourselves… and for all others wherever they may be, so that we may be found righteous by our life and actions, and faithful to the commandments, so as to obtain eternal salvation.
>
> When the prayers are concluded we exchange the kiss. Then someone brings bread and a cup of water and wine mixed together to him who presides over the brethren.
>
> He takes them and offers praise and glory to the Father of the universe through the name of the Son and of the Holy Spirit and for a considerable time he gives thanks that we have been judged worthy of these gifts.
>
> When he has concluded the prayers and

thanksgivings, all present give voice to an acclamation by saying: "Amen."

When he who presides has given thanks and the people have responded, those whom we call deacons give to those present the "Eucharisted" bread, wine and water and take them to those who are absent' (#1345).

The weekly readings and prayers from the Hebrew scriptures became seen by those present as being fulfilled in Jesus, and the bread and wine understood as a true sacrificial meal that enabled them to be sharers in the original sacrifice of the cross. This was a practice that could trace its source to the Jewish *Zebah Todah* (*Zebah* = 'sacrifice'; *Todah* = 'communion'), which had traditionally been offered in the Temple.[99]

There was no standard text in these early years for what we now call the 'Eucharistic Prayer' with individual celebrants being free, within limits, to compose their own versions and organise the overall ritual. As described by Pierre Loret, 'improvisation in liturgy at this time tended to be the rule rather than the exception'.[100] This would eventually give way to a more structured form of ministry due to the increase in numbers and also the emergence of a growing sense of

---

99 Pierre Loret, *The Story of the Mass: From the Last Supper to the Present Day* (Liguori Publications, 1982), p25.
100 Ibid, p40.

the sacred attaching to the office of those most closely associated with the Eucharist; a process that would lead eventually to the Church's rule on celibacy.

From the 3rd century onwards, specific examples of Eucharistic prayers began to emerge as the recommended material for general use. One of the earliest examples is found in a manuscript known as the *Apostolic Succession,* which is attributed to the priest Hyppolytus from around 215 AD. This describes the ceremony for the ordination of a bishop where the text is unmistakably the foundation of what is now our Second Eucharistic Prayer.

A later composition attributed to St Ambrose of Milan (died: AD 397) includes a prayer that is virtually word for word what became the 'Roman Canon' and which we now refer to as the First Eucharistic Prayer. The term 'canon' comes from the Latin word for rule and in respect of the Mass, the intention was for the celebrant to be obliged to recite a set authorised version of the prayer without changing anything in it.[101]

Special mention should be made of St Gregory (died: AD 604) who, following his election as Pope in AD 590, compiled the forerunner of our present missal by condensing several earlier writings together with corrections and clarifications. He was accused in some quarters of tampering with the 'apostolic prayer' to

---

101 Ibid, p53.

which his response was that there had never been such a prayer to begin with and that the mediocre scholarship of many of the texts in use made improvements essential.

It is also important to note that despite the patronage of several successive Popes, from the 5th century onwards, the use and application of the 'Roman Liturgy' remained relatively local for some time, with liturgical diversity being regarded as the norm and certainly the preference throughout Europe. The Roman liturgist seemed well aware that their indigenous formula could not simply be imposed, but required adaptation before adoption in order for people to see that what was being presented was a true reflection of their own tastes and customs.[102] One wonders whether Rome might ever consider readopting such an approach?!

As an altogether different issue, why did the Eucharistic ceremony come to be called 'the Mass'? The word is derived from the Latin word *missa,* meaning 'dismissal', which makes it an improbable choice of title as it says nothing about the mystery itself. It seems nevertheless to have emerged simply as a result of a general usage among the faithful and became accepted as the officially adopted title around the 5th century.

Centuries later, the Council of Trent (1545–63) issued two decrees on the nature, composition and purpose of the Mass in order to refute a number of

---

[102] Ibid, p68.

assertions that had been made by various Protestant Reformers. One of the decrees dealt with the act of transubstantiation and the focus of the other was the sacrificial reality of each Mass. Its understanding as a 'live re-enactment' of the death and resurrection of Jesus, not merely a form of service at which to recollect these past events. The Church acknowledged that the death and resurrection of Jesus was a once-and-for-all occurrence, but one which, by its nature, was forever 'engraved in the heavens and which overarches history', such that it can be present, and indeed *is* present, in our midst in all its redeeming power at every single Mass.

Whilst the Council of Trent assertively defended the traditional Catholic understanding of the Eucharist, one of the criticisms of its published findings is that it failed to fully connect the two decrees in order to present a more comprehensive appreciation of the Eucharist. In other words, a practice that can be found 'in the Church' but at the same time actually describes what is meant by 'being the Church'. In 1570, Pope Pius V produced a missal for the Mass with an express papal prohibition against any change and this was an edict that, for the most part, remained in force for almost 400 years until Vatican II.

Mass Today

I always find it a rewarding experience to attend Mass because of the magnitude of the event in which I believe I am participating. Unfortunately, I find the actual ceremony in its current 'authorised form' to be somewhat less inspirational.

I find it sad also that Mass seems to have become a proxy to determine what sort of Catholic a person is. Those who express an interest in a Latin Mass risk being thought of as theological reactionaries, whereas others who are not enthusiastic Latin Mass supporters might stand accused of not being a proper Catholic at all. In my experience, these arguments are generally confined to the externals of the Mass as if these alone determine its efficacy.

The Vatican II document on the Sacred Liturgy, *Sacrosanctum Concilium*, called for the pastors of the Church to ensure that the faithful take part in the ceremony 'fully aware of what they were doing, actively engaged in the rite and enthused by it' (SC #10). The Mass we celebrate today is the product of considerable historical research that was intended to add to people's understanding of what is entailed and to produce a ceremony to which they are better able to relate in their respective social and cultural environments.

I consider that *Sacrosantum Concilium* can be judged a success in setting out clear directional guidelines for us to follow. Our problem is the form and manner in which some of these guidelines have so far been implemented – if indeed they have been implemented at all. As a few personal reflections:

Language

The authorised rite of Mass is now generally celebrated in the vernacular. I can understand a sense of nostalgia for a Latin Mass in some quarters and a particular following for the music generally associated with Latin ceremonies, but I find it difficult to realistically imagine how the regular public prayer of the Church can ever be in anything other than the principal language of those who are participants.

The translation of the original Latin into English is the responsibility of an international committee of bishops (ICEL), which comprises eleven individual Bishops' Conferences from countries where English is the principal spoken language. However, their findings are subject to approval by a Rome-based Congregation for Divine Worship, which currently insists on 'formal equivalence' in English of whatever they consider to be the appropriate Latin base.

I referred earlier to the lack of a slavish literalness in the Gospel accounts of Jesus's words and actions at the Last Supper and surely this could be expected to apply similarly for modern liturgical translations. The priority is to convey the essential message, which is intended not simply to undertake a linguistic exercise in word substitution. I consider that the latest Rome-authorised English version of the Mass might, at best, be described as 'bland' and, as a result, serves to restrict the language's full potential to inspire and enthuse.

It is a situation that is made worse by insisting on a single authorised version for use in all English-speaking countries throughout the world. The Rome Congregation seem to be unaware that the approach to grammar and syntax, and the use of nuances and idiomatic expressions varies from country to country and influences the way in which the language continues to develop. Unlike Latin, English is a living language!

Scripture

Each Sunday we listen to an extract from one of the books of the *Old Testament* and this is followed by a psalm and two readings from the *New Testament*. The choice of individual readings follows a three-year rolling cycle in order to present a wide coverage of authors and content.

This is an arrangement that is wholly in accord with *Sacrosanctum Concilium*, which stressed the importance of Scripture and called for more varied and suitable readings to be adopted in order to generate a lively appreciation of their content (SC #35). However, for this to be effective, I consider it necessary for people to have at least a basic appreciation of the nature and background to the individual readings they are about to hear.

So, for example, rather than simply delivering a sequence of four readings and expecting a short homily to explain their interconnection, why not provide a brief 'introduction' to explain that particular Sunday's choice of readings; its biblical frame of reference and historical significance; the interconnection of the individual readings; and perhaps a brief biography of the respective authors and personalities being referred to. I am not suggesting a lecture course at each Mass, but in my experience people are inclined to listen more attentively (and constructively) if they have a general idea of what they can expect to hear and the reasons why.

I suspect that for many of the faithful, the readings at Sunday Mass represent their only weekly encounter with the Scriptures, which makes the method of presentation and the accompanying homily all the more important. Delivering homilies does not come easily to every pastor, but there are numerous readily available, well-structured and informative publications today that can be used or adapted for use.

The Eucharistic prayers

As a result of Vatican II, we now have a number of authorised Eucharistic prayers in addition to what was previously the sole 'Roman Canon' of the Mass and which used to be recited mainly in silence by the priest. In its present translated English form, it is referred to as the First Eucharistic Prayer, but I am not convinced that the latest 'authorised' translation is an improvement on what used to be the accompanying pre-Council

English version of the prayer – another casualty of Rome's present insistence on 'formal equivalence'.

It is evident that a significant amount of historical and biblical scholarship has been applied to produce these more recent compositions. But how widely is this appreciated within the Church and what is the general level of awareness of the origins and background of these several prayers? I cannot recollect a meaningful official explanation of the origins and composition of these several Eucharistic prayers we now use at Sunday Mass, and which I regard as a further missed opportunity for what could have been a productive series of homilies.

A consistent feature of the various new Eucharistic prayers that have emerged since Vatican II is the prominence they attribute to the workings of the Holy Spirit (*epiclesis*). I regard this as a highly significant feature that warrants greater emphasis by our pastoral leadership, together with an accompanying explanation. The workings of the Holy Spirit has generally been afforded greater prominence within the Orthodox Churches, but is an equally fundamental theological reality for us.

As for the rest of the sentiment to be found in the Eucharistic prayers, it is notable that in addition to prayers for the Pope and our own bishop as the focus of unity for each particular Church, the list now extends to refer to all auxiliary bishops, the Order of bishops, the clergy, deacons and the faithful as distinct classes which make up the People of God. The one exception is the Second Eucharistic Prayer, which omits any mention of the laity – that is, unless they are deceased!

Routine

The recent closure of church buildings as a result of Covid was accompanied by an assurance from our pastoral leadership that the 'obligation' of the faithful to attend Mass would be temporarily suspended without detriment. The use of the word obligation could seem to be indicative of how the hierarchy are still inclined to view Mass attendance.

For many people, attending Sunday Mass is what they have always been accustomed to do and an accompanying obligation was certainly a major consideration for Catholics of my generation. To some extent, this remains the case for this age group whereas younger Catholics require more convincing of what it is they are being asked to support and the reasons why.

If we return to first principles, we were asked by Jesus to come together as a community, to *'make real'* his life, death and resurrection in the manner in which he indicated. Sadly, I consider that the present authorised format for Mass frequently falls short of conveying this same heightened sense of being part of a 'live' re-enactment of these events and can often seem to be more in the nature of a routine (and compulsory) weekly testimonial, for the purpose of reminiscing a series of past events.

Mass is not for God's benefit, it is entirely for ours. It is an opportunity for each of us to come together with our unique set of joys, hopes and anxieties, and to place them in front of Jesus for him to make some sense out of them. In doing this, we can become increasingly aware of our connectedness to Jesus and also to each other as fellow human beings who are all present together at the same time, in the same place and for the same general purpose.

Mass in this sense is a therapeutic exercise. It is an opportunity for us to give thanks for who and what we are, to recharge our spiritual batteries (and sense of humour?!), and to remember family and friends who are no longer with us and others who may be experiencing difficult current circumstances. More importantly, we receive Jesus's gift of himself, which is freely given for our well-being, and it is because of all of this that we chose to keep coming to Mass. To leave people believing that attendance is principally in the nature of an ecclesial requirement or obligation is to seriously undervalue the whole ceremony.

The form of the Mass
I believe that Jesus is present with us in the bread and wine at Mass in the same way as he was present in the bread and wine at the Last Supper. At this first Mass,

he asked his disciples to 'do this' in his memory and so the question we need to ask today is how effectively do we think we are fulfilling his request?

I have attended a Mass and experienced a sense of being actively involved in a dynamic community re-enactment of the life, death and resurrection of Jesus – Maundy Thursday, Good Friday and Easter Sunday all in one. Attendance on other occasions has felt more like being just one of a number of people in an audience who just decided to attend a regular set-piece recital being performed by a nominated impresario.

These differing experiences will depend to some degree on one's own demeanour at the time, but this can be influenced by a number of the previously mentioned community factors, such as the form of greeting on arrival (or the lack of it!), the way in which the liturgy is introduced and conducted, and the level of participation that is encouraged. What we need to remember when planning our parish liturgy is who is the actual host, and from what we know about Jesus what form of ceremony and participation is he likely to wish to encourage?

This brings us to the 'rubrics' of the Mass – the authoritative rules of conduct for each liturgical service, which determine the sequence of actions to be performed by the celebrant as well as the reciprocal responses by the congregation. These are instructions that are issued and policed by Rome, so, for example, the congregation is required to stand at the entry of the celebrant and, for a sung Latin Mass, this could involve standing and sitting on up to thirteen occasions, accompanied by three required sessions of kneeling. Small wonder that Mass has attracted the sobriquet 'Sacred Gym'.

In order to begin the celebration of 'the sacred mysteries', we are called upon to admit that we have not simply sinned but that we have 'greatly sinned' and that this is due to our 'most grievous fault'. Do we really need to be confronted at the outset in this manner? We have come together because we know we are sinners and we attend Mass to reassure ourselves of God's unshakable love and forgiveness. I would have thought that this is a sufficient introduction to set the tone for our attendance and leave each individual to make their own reflections during the course of the liturgy.

I have previously mentioned the Bible readings at Sunday Mass, but if we add the prayer for the day (collect), the homily, the Credo and the bidding prayers, the congregation will have been subjected to eight separate pieces of information during the course of the first twenty-five to thirty minutes – not forgetting that they could have been required to stand and sit five times during this period. Might this, perhaps, be viewed as a potential overload?

As regards the 'bidding prayers', these were reintroduced to Sunday Mass following Vatican II. They follow a tradition that dates back to the early Church, which involved intercessions on behalf of individual persons or events and happenings of relevance to the community. They are of obvious benefit to their respective causes and collectively they enable the community at large to focus on the realities of their particular time and place.

Sunday Mass now frequently includes an offertory procession, which was again a custom in the early Church when gifts were brought and placed on the altar. Today's processions generally stop at the edge of the sanctuary and the gifts are taken to the altar by the celebrant or one of the altar servers. Perhaps I am being oversensitive, but this seems to at least hint at an imaginary line that has been drawn between the sanctuary as the designated sacred domain of the priests and the assumed regular place for the laity.

To return to the subject of language, St Luke's Gospel records that Jesus invited his disciples to address God as '*Abba*' or Father, and introduced them to a prayer that we now call the 'Lord's Prayer' or the 'Our Father' (Lk 11:1–4). The invitation is now described in 'formal equivalence' speech as, 'At the Saviour's command and formed by divine teaching we dare to say…', which seems to me to represent a somewhat stilted statement of intent rather than a personal invitation. Moreover, if this really is to be understood as a command, how could we dare not to follow it?

At the conclusion of the 'Our Father', we are invited to offer each other a sign of peace. This is a further restoration of an earlier custom and one I wholeheartedly support. It is otherwise possible to arrive at Sunday Mass as an individual and depart as an individual without any form of human interaction in between. Exchanging a sign of peace is, at least, an opportunity to secure an acknowledgement of one's existence.

I propose also to mention the vestments we use at Mass and raise the question of whether they are considered to be of help or hindrance in people's perception of the event? In my opinion, it could be more a case of the latter by further contributing to the view that most things involved with religion are a part of our past rather than our present or future. The chasuble takes its origin from the 'poncho' and in the early Church this would have been many people's usual form of dress until it began to take on a more elaborate form for those presiding at the Eucharist.

In my view, a specific form of attire for clergy (both on duty and off duty) is a practice that is more at home in the *Old Testament* as a means of distinguishing those who are connected with the altar and the Law (Mark 12:38–44). I consider that bishops should be given discretion to select liturgical vestments to suit the circumstances of their time and place, and which in our case might perhaps involve little more than adding a stole to normal modern attire for the celebrant at Mass – a stole being a reminder of the napkin used by Jesus when washing the feet of his disciples or, in any event, a symbol of his yoke of service.

As a general premise, I consider that anything that contributes towards evangelisation needs to be encouraged and anything that could detract from it should be modified or replaced. And as a corollary to the question of liturgical vestments in our own time, I have often wondered how the people of Jesus's time might have reacted to him and his message if he had chosen to travel around Galilea in jeans, trainers and a T-shirt?

It will be apparent that these several observations are not major theological issues, but in my view, their cumulative effect can influence a Mass's potential to enthuse. The theology of the Mass was established by Jesus when he instigated the Eucharist and there is nothing further we can add to this. Our role, with the help of his Spirit, is to ensure that his underlying purpose is transmitted to successive generations in a manner that continues to evoke their optimum response. Mass is not the product of any single time or place.

In order to achieve this, I consider that we should begin by setting the correct 'orientation' for the Mass. What I mean by this is that Mass often seems to replicate an *Old Testament* form of worship, which involves a wholly formalised ritual that is presented to appease a distant, omnipotent and judgemental God, pending the eventual arrival of a promised Messiah. Our belief is that Jesus is the Messiah and he specifically asked us to treat our dialogue and ongoing relationship with God in a personal manner as his adopted brothers and sisters, and in this way to narrow the previously assumed divide between God and humankind.

Jesus provided us with the essentials in order to reveal his intentions for our liturgy, and he did so without being prescriptive. We should take our lead from this by holding fast to what we believe to be the essentials, but focus on how best to 'represent' them in order to maximise their impact. This calls for a liturgy that takes account of the geography, the history and the culture of wherever Mass is to take place in order for it to again be seen and experienced as part and parcel of the fabric of people's everyday lives.

We now have the technology to 'stream' Mass. This was of immense benefit during the recent period of Church closures during the Covid pandemic, and it remains an ongoing blessing for the sick and the housebound. To be able to view Mass, combined with Holy Communion being brought to the home by a minister of the Eucharist, enables them to continue to feel part of their respective communities.

A streamed Mass is also an opportunity for those who may have ceased attending Mass to at least keep in touch with what is transpiring, and for regular members of the congregation it can be a necessary option of convenience from time to time. The questions are a) how many of the first group might be enthused by what they see and hear and become prompted to return to more regular Mass attendance? and b) could home viewing become the regular habit for a growing number of the faithful?

I believe the answer in both cases could depend to a great extent on what people see as the previously mentioned community aspects of welcome and participation by those present, over and above just observing a series of prayers and gestures. We need to try and replicate something of the atmosphere that would have been evident in the early domestic Masses, where friends, acquaintances and visitors alike were keen to come together to share each other's company and to participate in the Eucharist as a 'not to be missed' feature of their weekly routines. To be able to say 'I must go to Mass' meaning that it is an event that I do not wish to miss rather than it being a requirement or an obligation.

The Eucharist has been analysed, synthesised, packaged and dispensed over the centuries, but I wonder whether we have always been looking in the right place when seeking to measure its effectiveness? One thing that is certain is that to catch sight of Jesus at Mass, it is not necessary to always be looking heavenwards – he is clearly visible if and when we take the time to look around us at our fellow participants.

I will close with what I always consider to be an inspirational description of the Mass provided by Paul McPartlan:

> 'Overall, we may imagine local churches celebrating the Eucharist around their bishop, being woven together in a vast tapestry through time and across space by ties of apostolic succession and collegiality respectively which simply express the profound reality that, whenever the Eucharist is celebrated in any place at any time, only the heavenly mystery is present and one great purpose is at work: the one Christ is gathering the scattered children of God into the one Church… that these countless celebrations are not ultimately many but one. The integrity of the Church's witness to the Gospels demands that the oneness be evident.'[103]

---

103 Paul McPartlan, *The Sacrament of Salvation: An Introduction to Eucharistic Ecclesiology* (T&T Clarke, 1995), p67.

IN CONCLUSION

*'It is Jesus Christ alone we must present to the world.
Outside this we have no reason to exist.'*

This was the view expressed by Pope John Paul I, on the last day of his life in September 1978. One wonders where this may have led him, and indeed us, had his papacy not been so tragically short.

As it is, we do present Jesus to the world, but I consider that his message and example has become progressively subsumed within an extensively codified theology and set of ecclesial practices that are very much of our own making. In other words, we have institutionalised Jesus in order for him to fit our image and likeness, and this is 'the package' we are offering for people's intellectual assent and compliance.

Moreover, it is a package that is often presented in a manner that seems to call for a perpetual state of austerity or self-denial on our part as if these are the only means for us to make amends for our inherent sinfulness. And yet joy and happiness are God-given emotions that should connect us rather than isolate us from day-to-day life. It is through these emotions that we experience the world around us and come to see it as a source of revelation of God – the scale and the grandeur of our surroundings, the uniqueness of our individual presence, the love and fulfilment in our relationships, the satisfaction of giving and receiving, and so on.

This is a foretaste of what we believe is in store for us when we reach the fullness of God, not a competing agenda. We are the 'Easter People' who profess a belief in the risen Jesus who broke whatever fetters of sin may have existed previously and told us that he had come so that we would have life in full (John 10:10). We should believe Jesus, not just claim to believe *in* Jesus. Life is for living; sensibly and sensitively towards others, but not continuously looking over our shoulders for potential theological health hazards, which sometimes appears to be the only advice we receive from our pastoral leadership.

So how and why has such an attitude come about? In my view, one of the most likely explanations is that in seeking to preserve the message of Jesus, we have devised such an elaborate theological support apparatus over the years that we are sometimes inclined to focus on the apparatus as much as, if not more than, the message it is intended to convey, and to identify with the practices of the faith as much as the faith itself. We can become so immersed in ecclesial 'due process' that its preservation and protection, as well as the protection of everyone closely associated with it, becomes our primary objective. A situation that is all too sadly evident in the reported incidents of clerical sex abuse and accompanying attempts at an official cover-up.

To repeat one of the assertions contained in the *Catechism of the Catholic Church*, '…the Church has the mind of Christ' (#389), from which we seem to assume that we already have all of the answers and confuse our unity of faith with the notion of ecclesiastical conformity, where any question is treated as an act of dissent. As described by Gabriel Daley, the Church came to be thought of as resembling a village encompassed by a high wall, which both protected and also imprisoned the villagers with an effective system of taboos and cautionary tales in place to discourage them from venturing beyond the wall.[104]

Vatican II signalled a change of direction for Catholic theology and ecclesiology, or – to continue the above analogy – it breached the wall in several places and encouraged people to look outside. To understand also that they share, in their own way, in

---

104 Gabriel Daley, 'Faith and Theology' in *The Tablet*, April 1981, p361.

the one priesthood of Jesus and that the focus of all authority should be directed towards service. This is a combination of ideas and concepts that generates an altogether different Church environment, which will be exhilarating for some but could be disturbing for others who consider that the distinguishing feature of their faith and Church is authority as the remedy for all uncertainty.[105]

Generally speaking, the official Church response to current difficulties is to lay the blame solely on the growth of secularism in society and to attempt to close ranks against this and all other 'worldly philosophies' by pursuing the same doctrinaire approach and well-used religious agenda. We seem to have convinced ourselves that we hold the copyright on God and full performance rights for Jesus, and these combine to make us the 'perfect society' in what is an otherwise profane world.

In my view, the time has come for us to adopt a change of attitude and approach. As a starting point, we need to accept that in the context of God's eternal plan we are a means for this to become a reality; we are a sign of its presence in the world, but we are not the only means and we can never be more than a sign. We can never be the total embodiment of the eternal plan.[106]

---

105 Ibid, p361
106 Geoffrey Robinson, *Confronting Power and Sex in the Catholic Church* (The Columba Press, 2007), p78.

In terms of our role in proclaiming Jesus to the world, I consider that we should devote more time and effort to try to better understand how people relate to present Church teachings and their perception of religion in general, rather than simply assuming that we always know what is best for them. In my experience, individual worries or concerns arise, more times than not, due to a misunderstanding of what is actually being proposed or the implications that may arise as a result, and this is not helped by continually reciting the same litany of doctrinal 'sound bites'. I also believe that we could profitably revisit a number of the sound bites themselves, which, as currently presented, often seem to me to lack the benefits of modern biblical, theological and scientific scholarship.

In his book, *Tomorrow's Catholic,* Michael Morwood highlights the distinction between what he describes as our 'foundational belief' concerning God, Jesus and ourselves, and the various means we have at our disposal to help animate and sustain this belief. He lists our foundational belief as being:

> 'God is everywhere, loving and to be trusted absolutely.
>
> Jesus is divine and human and his way of living and loving shows us our potential as well as our destiny as human beings.

> We are sharers of the same Spirit of God that moved in Jesus. We are the body of Christ.
>
> As regards the means to sustain and expand our belief, we have stories (sacraments), teaching (doctrine), authority (laws), liturgy (prayer forms) and devotions (customs). The purpose of these features of Church experience is to continually point us towards our foundational beliefs and this is the primary criterion for us to evaluate their effectiveness for purpose.'[107]

Thus, in Jesus we become aware of our relatedness to God, who is not remote or demanding and does not require us to win His favour as each of us is already assured of God's unshakable love. Jesus himself is both divine and human and is therefore what we are if we take our inherent potential to its fullest level. An awareness of this and our call to be the body of Christ with him as our head is the 'Good News' offer we should be emphatically presenting.

Against this background, we need to seriously question stories that make us fearful of God or suggest that we have to earn God's mercy entirely by our own efforts. If teaching or preaching suggests, in any way, that Jesus is not really as human as the rest of us, it would represent a shift in our foundational belief.

---

[107] Michael Morwood, *Tomorrow's Catholic* (Spectrum Publications, 1997), p115.

And if what we believe about the real presence in the consecrated bread and our speculation on how that happens becomes more important than our belief in the real presence of the Spirit of God in the world, we would be losing focus on a fundamental truth about ourselves.[108]

It is, of course, important for us to retain safeguards in order to prevent the idea emerging of a god of soft indulgent love, a god so apparently loving that nothing is asked of people and they are challenged to nothing. Our current social environment, with its emphasis on relativism and political correctness, is particularly conducive to such a notion where the followers of this god can go so far as to deny the existence of right or wrong, personal responsibility or standards of conduct.

Our challenge is to maintain an outlook and an approach that avoids our foundational belief becoming submerged in excessive qualifications and conditions, or watered down by misguided novel concepts. In Hans Kung's most recent book, *Can We Save the Catholic Church?/We Can Save the Catholic Church!* he presents an interesting set of comparisons between a Church that is fashioned on the model of an 'absolute monarchy' and a Church more closely resembling the model propounded by St Francis of Assisi (1181–1225). His obvious reason for this particular comparison is

---

108   Ibid, p117.

that we now have a Pope called Francis, whose outlook could be said to be explicitly linked to his namesake from Assisi. This is used by Kung to highlight what he regards as three contrasting characteristics of Church:

Poverty
A monarchical Church suggests a Church of wealth, acquisitiveness and financial scandal, whereas the spirit of Francis suggests a Church of transparent financial policies and modest frugality. A Church that concerns itself, above all, with those who are poor, weak and marginalised, and acts to fight poverty and offers staff exemplary conditions of employment.

Humility
A monarchical Church can be a Church of power, domination, bureaucracy and discrimination. In contrast, a Church in the spirit of St Francis means a Church of humanity, dialogue, brother and sisterhood, hospitality for those who do not conform to prevailing norms, unpretentious service by its leaders, and a community that does not exclude new religious forces and ideas but allows them to flourish.

Simplicity
A Church in the monarchical mode can mean a Church of dogmatic immovability, moralistic censure and legal hedging; a Church where everything is regulated by

Canon Law; a Church of all-knowing scholasticism and of fear. A Church of St Francis means a Church of good news and of joy, and a theology based purely on the Gospel; a Church that listens to people rather than indoctrinating them from on high; and a Church that not only teaches, but constantly learns anew.

I am prompted to add a fourth characteristic, '*Honesty*', as although this should be implicit in everything we say and do, I consider that we are sometimes prone to adopting a 'selective presentation' of facts or a glossing over of detail when it comes to official pronouncements relating to the Church. It is a form of approach which is often reflected in teachings that can lead the individual to always assume that he or she must be wrong in questioning authority or the superiority of its wisdom, and by emasculating personal responsibility a person can be left not knowing what they think, only what they ought to think – and this is not necessarily the same thing at all.

The pomp and the ritual of ecclesiastical authority should never become a cloak for evasion, and Church rhetoric should not be used to obfuscate or dissimulate. So-termed 'higher interests' are no justification for deception, and ecclesiastical authority should not adopt a public manner that differs from its private manner.

To return to first principles, Jesus became incarnate in order for us to come to know God personally as our

Father. This is a concept I believe is perfectly expressed by Bishop Geoffrey Robinson:

> 'Our Christian faith is first and foremost faith in a person and the story of his life, death and resurrection and it is from this that other truths and behavioural indicators can flow. Without this personal relationship the truths will become lifeless, the norms of living will be burdensome tasks and the worship will be empty. With the relationship, the truths will come alive, the norms of living will be the most natural things in the world and the worship will be life-giving. Take the personal relationship out of religion and all that is left is an empty formalism.'[109]

I believe this is what we have allowed to happen and in order to begin to put this right, we need to admit that we do not yet hold the fullness of truth, nor are we able to make claims of absolute certainty for the poor human words we use to set out our understanding of the inner life of God and the exact manner in which Jesus is both divine and human. With God's grace, our level of understanding will continue to improve, but our priority should be to achieve a balance between clear statements of the beliefs we consider essential

---

[109] Geoffrey Robinson, *Confronting Power and Sex in the Catholic Church* (The Columba Press, 2007), p41.

for the identity of the Church and not attempting to place more detail and obligations on individuals than is necessary – it is an acceptable option 'to bow before the mystery of God rather than always attempting to define it'.[110]

An added difficulty we face at the present time is that a significant number of those in a position of authority in the Church appear oblivious to these issues or see no reason to consider anything other than current authorised policy. The often heard argument is that the Church has overcome problems in the past and will continue to do so again, even if this does result in a short-term shrinkage in numbers. I have no doubt that the Church of Jesus will prevail, but I find it difficult to support what is either the arrogance or the complacency in this sort of attitude.

Jesus appointed twelve of his disciples who, under the guidance of the Holy Spirit, were to be the means to provide guidance and support for the rest of his followers. The question is: was this appointment intended to comprise complete and exclusive control over every aspect of his message and over every fellow member of the people of God? Was the establishment of a hierarchy all that Jesus considered necessary in order to look after the Church until the end of time?[111]

---

110 Ibid, p238.
111 Referred to by Joseph Ratzinger, *The Ecclesiology of Vatican II* (Faith and Politics, 1988), p4.

I believe there are some within our pastoral leadership whose answer to such questions may well be 'yes' and this brings us to what I consider to be the principal 'fault line' in the Church today, namely the divide that has been allowed to develop between the ordained and the non-ordained, and the whole ecclesial system that has evolved around this.

The ordained exercise absolute control over all aspects of Church teaching and Church practices; they conduct their lives in a different manner to the rest of the baptised, they operate their own process for admissions and they pursue a highly regulated system for self-perpetuation. I consider that the unavoidable result of this approach is a collective mindset that is introspective and defensive in outlook and narrow in its application. It represents a model of Church that might in some ways be said to resemble the form of religious establishment in evidence at the time of the incarnation.

In my view, this is not what Jesus intended for his Church. It has come about as a result of confusing the concepts of ministry, priesthood and authority relative to his original message and example. It is an issue that we need to address, as the introduction of different classifications obscures the intended unity of one chorus of worship and does not simply damage the organisation of the People of God, but diminishes the force of the Gospel itself by weakening our understanding of the extent of Jesus's victory and the overwhelming nature of his gift to us as the Church.[112]

It is also an approach that is unlikely to continue to receive the support of the people in today's milieu. There is already a noticeable sense of disillusionment and frustration within the Church that a ruling 'clerical caste' operates entirely in accordance with its own agenda and is seen to be becoming increasingly remote and unresponsive to people's everyday needs and expectations. If a presumption in favour of continuing this form of 'two-tier' Church is a prerequisite to determine which candidates are likely to be selected to join the College of Bishops in the future, then I fear we could be approaching a potential 'tipping point' in terms of continued Church unity and membership retention.

In my view, we have failed to appreciate the full value of the insights that emerged from Vatican II, and a number of the Council's approved findings have themselves become surrounded by layers of ecclesial politics and protocol. In short, I consider that we are in a mess. It is a mess that is mainly of our own making and is therefore ours to resolve by means of prayer, charity and cooperation.

But for me, the most tragic consequence of our pastoral stewardship over the last sixty years, is that the

---

[112] Michael Richards, *A People of Priests: The Ministry of the Catholic Church* (Darton, Longman & Todd, 1995), p56.

Church is no longer automatically thought of as the ever present and ever welcoming 'home' to return to in order to find peace, comfort and reassurance. Many people are now inclined to look elsewhere for the life solutions they may be seeking.

My criticisms are directed against the existing 'Roman System' as opposed to particular individuals, but this is an all-pervasive system that seems to have inveigled successive generations of our pastoral leadership to imagine that the current, male-only celibate and authoritative model of Church Governance has been formed 'by divine teaching' and is not therefore ours to question – let alone attempt to change. I regard this as a misconception that needs to be rectified and time is not abundantly in our favour.

To end on a positive note, I am encouraged by a number of recent papal initiatives and our resultant direction of travel, to include the formal pronouncement on the *sensus fidei* and the revised eligibility criteria for Church governance.[113] These are features that have taken a little longer to come about than Pope John XXIII and Pope Paul VI may have envisaged at the time of the Council, but I firmly believe that the ever present support of the Holy Spirit will enable us to achieve 'the fullness of Charity' that we regularly pray for at each Mass.

---

113 Apostolorum Evangelicanus 2022.

CLOSURE

I began by acknowledging that I was a Catholic because this was the wish of my parents. I will end by expressing my gratitude to them for the choice they made on my behalf and also to record my appreciation of what this has meant for me as both a pre-Vatican II and a post-Vatican II Catholic.

Despite the strictures we were called upon to observe prior to the Council, as well as the abruptness or even the harshness in the way some of the teachings were presented, I can still look back to this period with affection. Catholicism in those days was a consciously present feature of our everyday lives with reminders of our religious heritage in the home, at family meals and family gatherings, in our schools, and in the regular round of parish Masses and social activities. They were experiences that combined to provide us with a strong sense of community and purpose.

The world has changed since then and so have we, with religion now tending to be treated as just one of a number of components in people's busy schedules, This does not diminish its underlying value and importance, and our task today is to express and give witness to our essential beliefs in ways that are suited to the times, rather than attempting to achieve a wholesale preservation of attitudes and practices from an earlier period. An exercise for which Jesus's parable of the old and the new wine skins seems highly pertinent (see Mk 2:18–22, Mth 9:14–17, Lk 5:33–39).

Many of my criticisms are directed towards our pastoral leadership, but in view of the all-pervasive position they presently occupy, this is unavoidable. However, my comments are intended to be constructive and are made with a sincere hope that they strike something of a responsive chord, and that under the guidance of the Spirit we can continue our journey as 'one body of Christ', and expand this beyond the purely written words of Vatican II.

In 2021, the whole of the faithful were invited by Pope Francis to express their view of what 'being Catholic' meant to them. The results are presently being processed and will form the agenda for a Bishops Synod due to take place in Rome later in 2023. This will be an opportunity to re-examine Vatican II with the benefit of sixty years' pastoral experience and it will hopefully enable us to plan our pastoral strategy for the next sixty years.

Predictably, the 'synodal process' has attracted criticism at both ends of the spectrum. There are those who regard the exercise as little more than a ruse, to allow the hierarchy to restate existing ecclesial guidelines by claiming that these continue to receive the support of a majority of the faithful. There are others who consider it an attempt to overthrow everything to which they have always been attached, in response to pressure from single-issue groups and movements within the Church.

In my view, we are privileged to have been participants in what is the most extensive and wide-ranging process of ecclesiastical discernment in Christian history. What remains for us now is to pray that the Spirit continues to guide the bishops and that they in turn will have the courage to respond in a positive manner to this latest example of the workings of the the *sensus fidei* of the whole of the people of God.

And for the future, that we can look forward to a Catholicism which we are all able enjoy and which attracts others to join us on our pilgrimage of faith.

BIBLIOGRAPHY

Audet, Jean-Paul, *Structures of Christian Priesthood* (Sheed & Ward, 1967)

Burns, Robert A., *Roman Catholicism after Vatican II* (Georgetown University Press, 2001)

Butler, Christopher, *In the Light of the Council* (Darton, Longman & Todd, 1969)

Castle, Tony, *Good Pope John and his Council* (Kevin Mayhew Publishers, 2006)

Congar, Yves, 'A Last Look at the Council' in Stacpoole, Alberic, ed., *Vatican II by those who were there* (London: Geoffrey Chapman, 1986)

Daly, Gabriel, 'Faith and Theology' in *The Tablet*, April 1981

de Lubac, Henri, *Catholicism: Christ and the Common Destiny of Man* (Ignatius Press, 1988) and *Theological Studies*, 1990

Duffy, Eamon, *Faith of Our Fathers* (Continuum, 2004)

Dulles, Avery, *Authority and Conscience* (Paulist Press, 1988)

Dyche, W., 'Transcendental Theology' in *Karl Rahner* (Liturgical Press, 1992)

Hill, Edmund, *Ministry and Authority in the Catholic Church* (London: Geoffrey Chapman, 1988)

Jaki, Stanley, *The Separation Between Science and Religion* (Real Time Books, 2002)

Kilby, Karen, *Karl Rahner* (Fount, 1997)

Komonchak, Joseph, 'Theology and Culture at Mid-Century: The Example of Henri de Lubac' in *Theological Studies,* Vol. 51, Issue 4, 1990

Kung, Hans, *Can We Save the Catholic Church?/We Can Save the Catholic Church.* (HarperCollins, 2013)

LaCugna, Catherine Mowry, *The Trinitarian Mystery of God* (Fortress, 1991)

Lightbound, Christopher, *The Church Then and Now: Memories and Reflections of a Parish Priest on the Turbulent Changes in the Church* (St Pauls, 2004)

Loret, Pierre, *The Story of the Mass: From the Last Supper to the Present Day* (Liguori Publications, 1982)

Lucas, Ernest, *Can We Believe Genesis Today?* (Inter-Varsity Press, 2001)

McPartlan, Fr Paul, *Eucharist: The Body of Christ* (Catholic Truth Society, 2004)

McPartlan, Paul, *The Sacrament of Salvation: An Introduction to Eucharistic Ecclesiology* (T&T Clark, 1995)

Morwood, Michael, *Tomorrow's Catholic* (Spectrum Publications, 1997)

Musto, Ronald G., *The Catholic Peace Tradition* (Orbis Books, 1986)

O'Collins, Gerald, *Jesus Our Redeemer: A Christian Approach to Salvation* (Oxford University Press, 2007)

O'Leary, Daniel J., *Lost Soul? The Catholic Church Today* (The Columba Press, 1999)

Ratzinger, Joseph: *The Ecclesiology of Vatican II* (Faith and Politics, 1998)

Richards, Michael, *A People of Priests: The Ministry of the Catholic Church* (Darton, Longman & Todd, 1995)

Riga Peter, 'The Ecclesiology of Johann Adam *Möhler*' in *Theological Studies* 22, 1961

Robinson, Geoffrey (Bishop), *Confronting Power and Sex in the Catholic Church* (The Columba Press, 2007)

Rosato, Philip J., 'Between Christocentrism and Pneumatocentrism: An Interpretation of Johann Adam *Möhler*'s Ecclesiology' in *Heythrop Journal* 19, 1978

Rush, Ormond, *Still Interpreting Vatican II* (Paulist Press, 2004)

Tanner, Norman P., *The Councils of the Church: A Short History* (Crossroad Publishing, 2001)

Wright, N.T., *Evil and the Justice of God* (SPCK, 2006)

Other references

A Catechism of Christian Doctrine (Catholic Truth Society, latest ed 1997)

Chapman, Geoffrey, *Catechism of the Catholic Church* (Continuum International Publishing, 1994)

Flannery, Austin, ed., *The Documents of Vatican Council II: Constitutions, Decrees, Declarations* (Newport, New York: Costello Publishing, 1966)

Glazier, Michael and Hellwig, Monika, ed., *The Modern Catholic Encyclopedia* (Dublin: Gill & Macmillan, 1994)

New Catholic Bible (Catholic Truth Society: 2007)

Made in the USA
Middletown, DE
16 January 2025